# 200 Years of First Presbyterian Church Columbus, Indiana

## Honoring Our Past, Building Our Legacy

BY PAUL J. HOFFMAN

*PathBinder Publishing LLC*
COLUMBUS, INDIANA

2024

Published by PathBinder Publishing LLC
P.O. Box 2611
Columbus, IN 47202
www.PathBinderPublishing.com

Copyright © 2024 by
Paul J. Hoffman
All rights reserved

Edited by Katharine Smith
Covers designed by Rachel McCarver
Front cover photo by Charles P. Day

First published in 2024
Manufactured in the United States

ISBN: 978-1-955088-76-3
Library of Congress Control Number: 2024943912

All rights reserved. No part of this book may be reproduced or transmitted in any form whatsoever without prior written permission from the publisher except in the case of brief quotations embodied in critical articles and reviews.

To all those who came before us who gave this congregation a solid foundation. To all those who are with us now, continuing to build the legacy. To all those who have been positively impacted by the good and faithful servants of this church.

**First Presbyterian Church**
512 Seventh Street
Columbus, IN 47201

**Phone**: (812) 372-3783
**website**: https://www.fpccolumbus.org

**Mission statement:**

To be an active, growing, inclusive and caring church family that witnesses to God's love and shares the good news of Jesus Christ. Our mission leads us to invite all people to participate fully in our community and worship life as safe, loved, and accepted children of God, including:

- Conventional Christians and questioning skeptics
- Children and adults of all ages
- People of all sexual orientations and gender identities
- People of all races and cultures
- People of all socioeconomic situations
- People of all mental and physical abilities
- Those who bring hope to the world and those who seek hope

200 YEARS of FIRST PRESBYTERIAN CHURCH of COLUMBUS, INDIANA

# Introduction

**Perhaps the** Rev. Ninian S. Dickey summarized best why we should learn from the past when he addressed the congregation the day after the current building was dedicated in 1875. His speech, which focused mainly on the roughly 50-year history of First Presbyterian Church of Columbus up to that time, led off with the reasons that looking back was so important.

He started, "– Deuteronomy 8:2. Thou shalt remember all the way which the Lord thy God led them."

Dickey, the son of the minister who had helped charter this church on July 3, 1824, and who had pastored First Presbyterian for nearly 18 years before leaving in 1870, also included in his speech the following remarks relating to the importance of remembering the past:

"If the events of the past are burried [sic] in the waste of ages, there are no landmarks by which to trace the track of time, and no means of understanding the influences which have moulded [sic] human destiny.

"Lessons of wisdom are learned and fixed in the mind which will be of great advantage, for it is by review and repetition that memory becomes retentive, and the past as though the present.

"How much happiness, too, does a retrospective view give us, if our actions have at all been worthy of immortal beings; and if time has been misspent or wasted, how well calculated to awaken regrets and lead us to repentance and reformation.

"The great obligation of human existence is a preparation of right action and a true course of life. That we act rightly in the future, we must live rightly now. The true principles and pathway of success, the dangers that beset that path, all that forearms and forewarns, may be drawn from the facts of the past; for it is the power of looking back on past experience that gives us the power of foreseeing the future, and thus of looking both before and behind us for sources of enjoyment and for a true direction in the moral course of life."

---

"It is the power of looking back on past experience that gives us the power of foreseeing the future."

— Ninian S. Dickey

# 200 YEARS of FIRST PRESBYTERIAN CHURCH of COLUMBUS, INDIANA

It is in the spirit of Dickey's speech that we endeavor at the 200-year mark in our history (what we believe to be the longest tenure for a church without changing its denomination in Bartholomew County) to look back, so that we may learn lessons from the past that will help us act rightly in the future.

In looking back, we explain how this congregation rose from the humblest beginnings in the Indiana wilderness and how the early members overcame struggles to keep the congregation together. We explain how First Presbyterian navigated such traumatic events as the Civil War, the fight for rights for marginalized sectors of society, the rise of the Ku Klux Klan, the COVID pandemic and more. We also tell the stories of the multitude of social justice programs that started with this church and its members.

As such, this book honors our past. But we also want this book to play a part in the efforts we still undertake to build upon our legacy. With that in mind we hope you get a sense of not only where we've been, but also where we are now and where we plan to go from here. Those plans include continuing to advocate for and serve the same people Jesus spent so much of his ministry serving … those on the fringes of society.

The Rev. Dr. Felipe Martinez and his wife, Tracy Heaton de Martinez, in front of the church at Seventh and Franklin streets.

"The son of man did not come to be served but to serve."

— Mark 10:45

First United Presbyterian Church

# Acknowledgments

**This book**, *200 Years of First Presbyterian Church Columbus, Indiana: Honoring Our Past, Building Our Legacy*, would not have come together as quickly as it did had Carol Berkey and her crew not done such an awesome job putting our 175th anniversary book together in 1999. Much of the information contained in this book stems from that effort. Parts of the 175th book are reprinted here verbatim; parts were expanded upon to give you an even deeper sense of our history.

Paul J. Hoffman, a current member of First Presbyterian, headed the 200th anniversary book effort. An author and publisher, he conducted roughly a dozen interviews with longtime members and others to compile information on the past 25 years. He also researched everything he could from the first 175 years, making (very few) corrections to the previous book and adding details to the stories. The main outside sources he used were the Bartholomew County Historical Society, the Bartholomew County Public Library, *The (Columbus) Republic*, Newspapers.com, and other online sites. Besides the 175th book, previous church histories by John Scott, the Rev. Ninian S. Dickey, Carrie Ong, Ross Crump and others also proved useful.

We owe a big thank you to Carol Berkey, who wrote the 175th anniversary book for First Presbyterian.

Rachel McCarver, co-chair of the Bicentennial Committee, designed the front and back covers.

Katharine Smith, a longtime member and retired copy editor at *The Republic*, provided copy editing.

Carol Rumple spent countless hours organizing boxes upon boxes of church historical records. The foundation gave funding to get the book published.

Many others contributed, whether they knew it or not, especially members of our Bicentennial Committee, who provided much needed knowledge and encouragement.

There is much more to the story of this church and its members (especially their contributions outside of First Presbyterian) that could be told in this volume. We ask forgiveness for not being able to include more but thought had to be given to the number of pages and the resulting cost to the purchaser, as well as deadlines.

We do wish to offer one last big thank you ... to everyone who has been so supportive of not only this book effort but also of this congregation – past, present and future – and the community it continues to serve.

200 YEARS of FIRST PRESBYTERIAN CHURCH of COLUMBUS, INDIANA

# Table of Contents

A Congregation is Born ............................................................... 8
John M. Dickey, Organizing Minister ....................................... 11
Our Founders ............................................................................. 14
Our Early Days .......................................................................... 20
Constructing Our Current Building ......................................... 29
A Parade of Pastors ................................................................... 35
The Alexander E. Sharp Sr. Era ................................................ 42
Following in Father's Footsteps ................................................ 46
Bill Laws: A Giant of a Man ..................................................... 54
A Growing Congregation in a Growing Community ............. 68
A Major Building Project and Our First Female Ministers .... 82
The 21st Century ..................................................................... 110
Our Bicentennial ..................................................................... 126
Our Future ............................................................................... 128
Our Ministers .......................................................................... 131
About the Author ................................................................... 132

200 YEARS of FIRST PRESBYTERIAN CHURCH of COLUMBUS, INDIANA

# A Congregation is Born

**First Presbyterian Church** in Columbus, Indiana, traces its roots to before the official chartering of the congregation 200 years ago. But not by much. White settlers had just started moving to the area a few years prior, and the first recorded instance of Presbyterians coming together to hear a preacher was in the summer of 1822, just over a year after Columbus and Bartholomew County were born.

At the time of the Presbyterians' first meeting, the state of Indiana was 6 years old, and its capital was still in the southern city of Corydon; it wouldn't move to Indianapolis until 1825.

The Columbus area in the 1820s featured fertile soil but little else to recommend it. As historian Williamson H. H. Terrell wrote of the area: "The numerous rivers and creeks were fouled and obstructed with fallen timbers, drifts and other accumulation of vegetable debris. The waters from freshets and overflows stood reeking and stagnant in the lowlands and in the sloughs and bayous, and gave out their noxious

Left: Clearing an Indiana forest. Right: An early log home in Bartholomew County. // Bartholomew County Historical Society

# 200 YEARS of FIRST PRESBYTERIAN CHURCH of COLUMBUS, INDIANA

exhalations for miles and miles around, while thick forests and tangled undergrowth in rank and profuse verdure almost equalled [sic] the famed valley of the Amazon."

Disease was rampant, especially in the fall of the year, when many inhabitants fell ill with ague, a malarial disease. "Whole settlements at times were struck down and rendered almost helpless," Terrell wrote.

Despite this, the area grew, although slowly. Lured by the rich soil, families began to migrate here. The Hawpatch and Clifty regions were said to be among the finest and richest in the state. Among all this sat Columbus (originally platted as Tiptona), a crude frontier village set on a rise on the east bank of the East Fork of the White River, at the confluence of the Flat Rock and Driftwood rivers. By 1822, a few log cabins had been built here, and some families had purchased land and were starting to settle in the area.

It was in this wilderness that a small group of Presbyterian pioneers met in a two-story frame house owned by Thomas and Elizabeth Hinkson to listen to the preaching of John M. Dickey, a missionary of the Presbyterian Board of Domestic Missions. The house was located just south of the public square, and a meeting room was improvised on the first floor by use of a few planks resting on chairs at either end.

It was not the easiest place in which to build a congregation.

Dickey's son, Ninian S. Dickey, who would serve as the Presbyterian congregation's pastor from 1853 to 1870, said the early village that would someday be known as "The Athens of the Prairie" was "a hard place morally" due to the influence of alcohol and a few lawless men. In those days, a "big bellied bottle" of whiskey was said to have been kept standing upon the table during sessions of the Board of County Commissioners in the courthouse, open to whoever wished to partake. Father Haven, a presiding elder of the Methodist church here, stated it bluntly, when he said, "The devil has a bill of sale for Columbus."

Williamson Terrell, also a Methodist minister, said that at the time liquor was considered a necessity to "fortify the system" against the negative effects of the bad water and hardships of life in the woods. Many families ingested a strong drink called "bitters" before breakfast to help ward off ague and malarial diseases. The practice did lead to widespread intemperance, Terrell said, against which all churches took a strong stand. In response to a feud, he'd been having with a politically powerful and unscrupulous family, Terrell carried a knife for fear of reprisals.

Still, Presbyterians and worshippers of other denominations marched onward. For the next two years, Presbyterians met at each other's homes at irregular periods, worshipping together. On July 3, 1824, 17 of these pioneers met at what was likely an old brick courthouse in the center of the public square, organizing into the Presbyterian Church of Columbus under the authority and direction of the Rev. Dickey. There is no record of the official location of that meeting, but the two-story courthouse, built the year before at a size of 40-by-40 feet, was said to be the only building large enough to accommodate all who attended.

At the time, Columbus was a village covering some 40 acres, bounded on the north by Fifth (then Harrison) Street, on the east by the alley behind Lafayette

---

*"It was in this wilderness that a small group of Presbyterian pioneers met in a two-story frame house owned by Thomas and Elizabeth Hinkson to listen to the preaching of John M. Dickey, a missionary of the Presbyterian Board of Domestic Missions."*

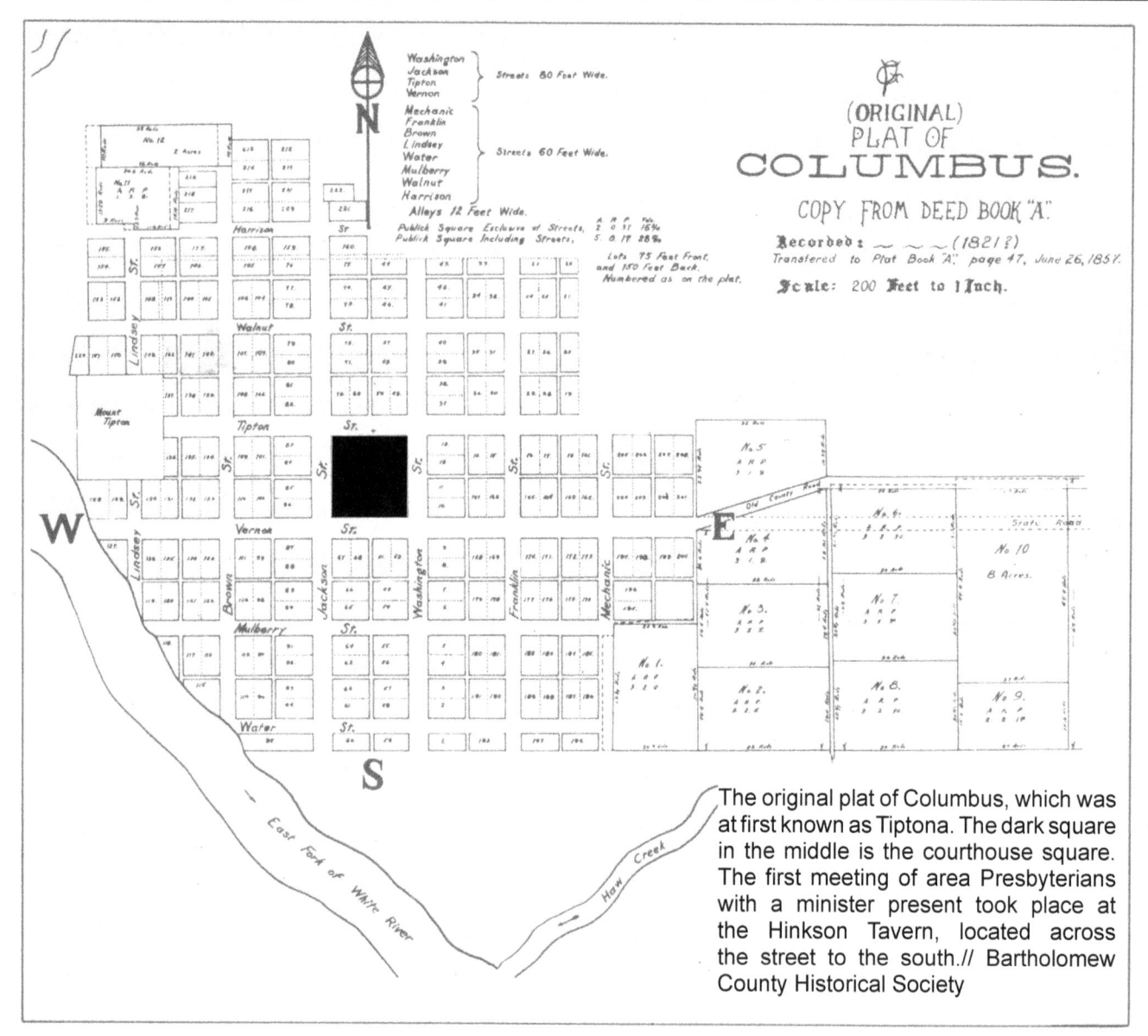

# 200 YEARS of FIRST PRESBYTERIAN CHURCH of COLUMBUS, INDIANA

The original plat of Columbus, which was at first known as Tiptona. The dark square in the middle is the courthouse square. The first meeting of area Presbyterians with a minister present took place at the Hinkson Tavern, located across the street to the south. // Bartholomew County Historical Society

Avenue (then Mechanic Street), on the west by the river and the south by what would now be roughly First Street. The houses were mostly log structures, and except for the courthouse, there were no buildings suitable for worship by any congregation until 1831.

Upon chartering, the congregation named Joseph Hart elder. Father Dickey came to serve the congregation when he could, sometimes only once a year. Communion and baptisms had to wait until an ordained minister could administer the sacraments. Yet the church held together.

SOURCES:
"The Land Which Your Fathers Possessed," Dec. 30, 1905.
First Presbyterian Centennial Week program, 1924
Berkey, Carol, *First Presbyterian Church: A History*, 1999.

# John M. Dickey, Organizing Minister

**First Presbyterian Church** in Columbus was one of several churches founded by John McElroy Dickey, "the father of Presbyterianism in Indiana." He was one of eight ministers present at the first Synod of Indiana meeting, Oct. 18 to 21, 1826, and in fact preached the sermon at that meeting. [1]

But he had been active in Indiana well before that.

Dickey, of Scottish-Irish descent, was born Dec. 16, 1789, in York County, South Carolina, to David and Margaret Stephenson Dickey. The oldest of six children, Dickey made his way to Kentucky and married Nancy W. McCluskey in October 1813, in Livingston. She died, and Dickey married Margaret "Peggy" Osborne Steele in 1818 in Washington, Indiana. Between the two wives, he fathered 13 children, though two died in infancy.

Dickey was the first installed minister in Indiana, first at the White River Church near Washington Church in 1819, but he carried on his missionary work and then the Lexington throughout his long ministry, traveling by horseback as far north as Crawfordsville. In 1824 alone, he organized three Presbyterian churches, including the one in Columbus.

Circuit riders made the rounds, usually on horseback, to serve congregations. John McElroy Dickey, "The father of Presbyterianism in Indiana," was the circuit rider who helped charter First Presbyterian Church of Columbus on July 3, 1824.// General Commission on Archives and History for the United Methodist Church, Drew University.

"I am told that father read the Bible all the way through at the age of four," his son, Ninian S. Dickey, later wrote. "I am not sure that even I believe that, but the story does demonstrate what an ardent and dedicated student he was."

He chose the name "McElroy" as his middle name to honor the McElroy family, who took him in when he arrived after traveling 250 miles through Kentucky at the age of 18 or 19 to attend a new school, Ninian said.

Much is known about how and when the early Presbyterian churches were planted here, in addition to Dickey's efforts to raise churches and a family in Indiana from his short manuscript, "History of the Presbyterian Church in Indiana," published in 1828 under the direction of the Salem

---
1 Woodburn, James Albert. "Pioneer Presbyterianism." *Indiana Magazine of History Vol. XXII*, December 1926.

# 200 YEARS of FIRST PRESBYTERIAN CHURCH of COLUMBUS, INDIANA

Presbytery. That book was cited as being a major source of information in forming the address at the centennial celebration of the Indiana Synod in Vincennes in 1926.

That address, given by James Albert Woodburn, emeritus professor of American history at Indiana University, included much information about Dickey, which is retold below.

Dickey's education was the result of his hard labor. He studied theology in Kentucky with Dr. Nathan H. Hall. He was licensed to preach in 1814 by the Muhlenburg Presbytery when he was 25. "Presbyterians, with their insistence on educated pastors who would be paid for their services, were not popular on the frontier," according to Ninian. "But Father, being a frontiersman from Kentucky himself, was accepted and welcomed among the settlers."

In December 1814 Dickey visited Indiana at Washington, where a church had been established not long prior. Indiana was still a territory, and when he came, there were only two other organized Presbyterian societies, at Vincennes and Charleston.

He returned to Kentucky but in May 1815 came back to Indiana with his wife and baby girl. The family and all their earthly goods were carried on the backs of two horses. His library consisted of a Bible, Buck's "Theological Dictionary," Bunyan's "Pilgrim's Progress," and Fisher's "Catechism." When Dickey paid for the ferry for the family to cross the Ohio River, he had only 25 cents left.

The people were as poor as he, and they could not afford to pay a minister much, if anything. Dickey supported his family by farming, teaching and writing deeds, wills and advertisements. He knew how to farm; he cleared 30 acres, and his crops were abundant. He kept close account, and his average salary for the first 16 years in Indiana, including money and gifts, was $80 a year (equivalent to about $2,500 today).

Dickey preached every Sabbath and oftentimes during the week. After four years' service in Daviess County, he moved to New Lexington (also called Lexington) in Scott County in 1819 and became the pastor of the churches there and at New Washington (Clark County), becoming the first installed Presbyterian pastor in the state. He also took charge of Graham Church on Graham Creek in Jennings County.

In 1823, the Assembly appointed him to the Committee of Missions. Dickey made a tour to Vincennes and Crawfordsville, scattering announcements and filling appointments as he went. His figure was spare and bent, yet on this journey he preached 31 sermons in 30 days, "a living exemplification of the adage 'a lean hound for a long race.'" The rains had fallen, the Wabash River and its tributaries were swollen. There were few, if any, bridges. But as he said, "the Lord delivered me out of deep waters."

In 1824 he spent two months in the counties of Batholomew, Rush, Shelby and Decatur, during which time he organized the churches of Columbus, Franklin and New Providence, between Franklin and Shelbyville in Shelby County (now First Presbyterian in Shelbyville).

He is credited with organizing six Presbyterian churches in southern Indiana and encouraging many others, serving as a sort of rural bishop and a perpetual missionary. After the organization of the Presbyterian church in Columbus, he supplied it at one time for six months, one Sunday a month. For many years, he came once a year, holding meetings for several days, baptizing children, receiving members into the church and administering Communion. He was present at every Communion season for many years, preaching here as late as 1842.

> "Was there ever greater faith or greater faithfulness in Israel than Dickey's in his pioneer service?"
>
> — James Albert Woodburn, historian

Much of his success can be attributed to his wife, through whose Herculean efforts 11 children were raised. She often lived alone with the children for months at a time, while their father was away on long, laborious missionary journeys. It was said she was excellent with the spinning wheel and loom and made all the family's garments for years. She became quite a scholar and taught her children and, eventually, neighbors' children.

Father Dickey died Nov. 21, 1849. He was only 60, but his wiry frame had worn itself out. The hardships of frontier life were not conducive to longevity. When the Synod met at New Albany a few weeks before his death, he wrote to his brethren telling them of his feebleness and assuring them that his work was nearly done. Upon receiving a reply, Dickey was deeply moved, and at the family altar with choked utterance, he gave thanks to God that the lines had fallen to him in such pleasant places, among such loving and faithful brethren.

"It is service to others that makes the heart tender and grateful," Woodburn said. "Was there ever greater faith or greater faithfulness in Israel than Dickey's in his pioneer service?"

He is buried, along with his wife, Margaret, at Britan/Pisgah Cemetery east of New Washington. A plaque at the cemetery dedicated on November 21, 1938, honors him. It was "erected by grateful admirers to perpetuate as history and landmarks the old Dickey Homestead nearby, and this graveyard, where rest the mortal bodies of this man of God and his faithful wife."

SOURCES:
Berkey, Carol. *First Presbyterian Church: A History*, 1999.
Dickey, John M. "History of the Presbyterian Church in Indiana," (1828, Salem Presbytery)
"The Land Which Your Fathers Possessed," Dec. 20, 1905.
Edson, Hanford A. *Early Presbyterianism in Indiana*, 1898.
First Presbyterian Centennial Week program, 1924.

## 18th and Early 19th Century Worship

*Provided by the Department of History, PC USA, in Montreat, North Carolina.*

- The congregation had no verbal part in the service except for singing.
- The minister usually did not wear a robe. The choir did not wear robes.
- Sermons often lasted 1 to 3 hours.
- In the 1700s the congregation stood for the prayers, stayed seated for singing of psalms/hymns. This was reversed by the mid-1800s.
- By the early 1800s organs were becoming popular in larger churches and were often used in the more revival style of worship services practiced by the "New School" faction of Presbyterians.
- There was no separate choir during the 1700s; however, by the turn of the century, the use of choirs increased due to the constantly changing tune books that were being approved by the General Assembly-(s). Congregations found it hard to keep up and left a lot of singing to the choir.
- In the 1800s it became common to pass a hat or plate or use collection bags on long poles for the offering instead of having a collection box at the exits.
- Women did not serve as elders or ministers in the 1800s.
- Printed Orders of Worship came later.
- The pulpit and Bible would be located at the center of the chancel.
- The use of a Beadle to bring in the Bible and carry it out at the end is from our Scottish heritage.

# 200 YEARS of FIRST PRESBYTERIAN CHURCH of COLUMBUS, INDIANA

# Our Founders

**On July 3, 1824**, a congregation of 17 members was officially chartered, with the Rev. John M. Dickey as installing minister. The charter members were Joseph and Mary Hart, David and Kezia Hager, Abner and Betsy Mounts, Edwin and Cynthia Brown, Samuel and Ruth Makinson, Elizabeth Hinkson, John Henry, Martha Gabbert, and Andrew and Sarah Rogers with their daughters, Jane and Mary Ann.

Those received by letter were the Harts, Hagers, Rogerses, Betsy Mounts, John Henry, Cynthia Brown, Elizabeth Hinkson and Ruth Makinson. The others were received on profession of faith.

A few days later, the congregation grew to 20 with the addition of Sarah Snyder, Maria Wiles and Sarah Farmer.

Among that group featured a Revolutionary War veteran who carried in his right hip a British minnie ball the rest of his life, a young man whose father was convicted of murdering his mother and escaped from an Ohio prison, and a woman whose husband led a company of spies during the War of 1812.

The grave sites of First Presbyterian founding members, Joseph Hart and his wife, Mary Hart, at Garland Brook Cemetery in Columbus.// Paul J. Hoffman photo

Here are profiles of our founders:

**Joseph and Mary Hart**

Joseph Hart's journey from serving as a substitute soldier for the United States against England to one of our founders, and presumably our most stalwart leader of the infant Presbyterian church here, is an intriguing one.

Hart was born in Loudon County in northern Virginia on June 16, 1761. His parents were Thomas and

14

Nancy Stout Butler Hart, both Presbyterians of Scottish-Irish descent who came to America from Wales. Hart's parents died while he was an infant, and a kindly Christian neighbor cared for him until he was 16 years old.

In early 1777, Hart's foster father was drafted into the U.S. Army, but Hart offered to go in his place and served in Capt. John Holcombe's company of the Fourth Virginia Regiment. Hart was discharged on Feb. 16, 1778, after having been wounded in battle near Guilford Courthouse, South Carolina. He'd been hit in the right hip by a musket ball that was never extracted. When he was nearly 70 years old, Hart was offered a pension for his Revolutionary War service, but despite having been wounded in service, he declined, saying "I did very little service for the country. The government is now in debt, and I cannot ask for money."

Hart's Christian principles led him to detest human slavery, and he moved to two different areas in Virginia to get away from slave-owning plantations.

In 1788 in Washington County, southwest Virginia, he married Nancy Shanklin. They had a son, but within two years the number of slave-owners had increased so much that Hart and his family headed west to Tennessee.

Hart united with other settlers in Maryville, Tennessee, building a fort named Old Fort McTeer to fend off Cherokee and Creek raids.

It was about 1796 that Joseph Hart made a public profession of his religion and united with the New Providence Presbyterian Church in Maryville. Soon afterward, he was made an elder and clerk of session in the church.

Hart's wife died in 1807 after a short illness, leaving five sons and a daughter in her husband's care. Two years later, he married Mary Means, whose Presbyterian parents had immigrated to the United States from the north of Ireland in 1790 to escape religious persecution. Hart and his second wife had five sons, giving him a total of 10 sons and one daughter, though not all survived childhood.

Hart was a teacher and a farmer in Tennessee, and he served his community as a teamster, taking produce to the gold mining region in Georgia and cotton to Baltimore and bringing salt to the community from salt mines in southeastern Kentucky. At one time, he was a magistrate of the county court and was occasionally an American Bible Society volunteer. One of his sons stated that Joseph Hart "was always in the saddle."

Tennessee had become a slave state in 1796, and as more citizens there acquired slaves, the less Joseph Hart felt welcome. In spring 1820, his son, Gideon Blackburn Hart, went to Indiana, eventually proposing the family move to Bartholomew County. In the middle of September 1821, the Hart family left Tennessee in two wagons pulled by two horses apiece. They had a large tent, two cows and an extra saddle horse that Joseph Hart rode.

Gideon, who by this time was staying in Vincennes, met his family at the Cumberland Gap and accompanied them to a spot five miles east of Columbus near Clifty Creek. The trip from Maryville to their new home took the Harts four weeks and included their four surviving children, ages 9 years to 18 months, and two of Joseph's older children. Their purchase of 160 acres cost them $2 per acre.

For six weeks of an Indiana winter the family lived in a tent while the older sons felled trees and cut logs. At last neighbors came to erect a log cabin in a day's time. Sons and neighbors also built a stable, dug a well, and cleared and fenced 12 acres, having it ready to plant corn, flax and potatoes by the following May. There was an abundance of wild game nearby. However, "Joseph Hart was so much opposed to hunting, because it encouraged an idle, shiftless life, that he would not have a gun in the house."

# 200 YEARS of FIRST PRESBYTERIAN CHURCH of COLUMBUS, INDIANA

Shortly after arriving, Hart began to meet with other area Presbyterians, and they expressed a desire to charter a congregation. When First Presbyterian of Columbus was officially chartered, Hart was named ruling elder, and for many years he was the church's only official. He also served as clerk of sessions from 1824 until his death in 1841. In 1826, the first Sabbath school in the county was held at the Hart cabin.

After a two-year illness, Joseph Hart died June 20, 1841, at the age of 80. He was buried in Sand Hill Cemetery in Clay Township, where he was joined by his wife and son. When what was then State Road 46 (now 25th Street) was straightened east of Columbus, these three graves, along with two others, were moved to Garland Brook Cemetery.

"Presbyterianism in this region and Christianity owe a great deal to this godly man," Ninian S. Dickey wrote of Joseph Hart. "When I came to this place, his consistent and laborious Christian life was an almost constant theme for conversations by Christians of this region, of every denomination ...

"Scarce a week passed during my residence here, but some influence for good was seen to have descended from Father Joseph Hart."[1]

The local chapter of the Daughters of the American Revolution is still named for him.

## Elizabeth Hinkson

While Elizabeth (Foose) Hinkson was a founding member of the church, her husband, Thomas, being a Methodist, was not. However, Thomas was also instrumental in the early meetings of the congregation. It was by his hands that the first frame structure in this town was built, and that building provided a meeting place for local Presbyterians.

The son of Irish immigrants, Thomas Hinkson was born in 1772 in Westmoreland, Pennsylvania. In the autumn of 1790, as a volunteer in the Kentucky militia, he was part of a United States Army mission to subdue confederated Native American nations near Fort Wayne. In this battle, he received a slight wound in the left arm and narrowly escaped with his life. Previously a private, Hinkson earned the rank of lieutenant after the battle despite never pretending he had done anything worthy of distinction that day.

He returned to Harrison County, Kentucky, married Elizabeth Foose in 1794, and settled on a farm. In spring 1806, he moved to southwest Ohio and soon afterward was elected a justice of the peace for Highland County and captain of the militia company to which he belonged. When Clinton County was formed in 1810, without his knowledge he was elected by the legislature one of the first three associate judges for the new county. He made no pretensions to legal knowledge, just that he had good common sense.

He continued to farm. He felt an obligation to return to active duty when the U.S. declared war against Great Britain in June 1812 over territorial disputes. Hinkson was one of the two men chosen to lead a company of spies, named Hinkson's Mounted Spies. Due to his brave and daring efforts during the war, upon his return home Hinkson was immediately elected colonel of the Third Regiment of the Second

> "Presbyterianism in this region and Christianity owe a great deal to this godly man (Joseph Hart). When I came to this place, his consistent and laborious Christian life was an almost constant theme for conversations by Christians of this region, of every denomination."
>
> — Ninian S. Dickey

---

1 "Historic Discourse of the Presbyterian Church of Columbus, Indiana. *The Columbus Republican*, Jan. 7, 1875.

> "Mr. Abbett came there (Hinkson's tavern) to preaching one Sunday, and afterwards to board at my mother's. He was a tailor, and the house had a bar room; but my mother was always opposed to whiskey, so she rented this bar room to Mr. Abbett for a 'tailor shop.' Church was held in this room on Sunday; mother let every denomination preach there."
>
> — Margaret Hinkson Abbett
> Daughter of Thomas and Elizabeth Hinkson

Brigade and First Division Ohio militia, a post of some honor.

"He was a plain, gentlemanly individual, of a very mild and even temper; a good husband and kind father, but rather indifferent to his own interest in money matters, by which he became seriously involved, lost his property and moved to Indiana in 1821."

Hinkson included a bar when he built a tavern near the public square, but his wife was so opposed to drinking that she gave the bar room to one of her boarders, a tailor, for his shop. Hinkson also operated a ferry service over the Driftwood River near his home and was named an associate judge of the county court in November 1822. Court sessions were on occasion held at his home.

He died in 1824 at the age of 52; the exact date is unknown.

Elizabeth, meanwhile, was born in Tennessee in 1777 and died in 1858 in Bartholomew County.

The couple's daughter, Margaret Hinkson Abbett, later wrote of life at the tavern: "There was a whiskey shop right across the street from my mother's house, and she told us five girls that we must not go near there, for the devil was there where they played the fiddle, and of course, we were afraid."

There was always preaching in the house, including by Margaret's future husband, the Rev. John B. Abbett.

"Mr. Abbett came there to preaching one Sunday, and afterwards to board at my mother's. He was a tailor, and the house had a bar room; but my mother was always opposed to whiskey, so she rented this bar room to Mr. Abbett for a 'tailor shop.' Church was held in this room on Sunday; mother let every denomination preach there.

"I was married to Mr. Abbett in the bar room of our house, which was afterward burned down."

**David and Kezia Hager**

David Hager was born in Washington County, Maryland, on Sept. 7, 1780. He was married twice, first to Margaret Keller. After her death, he married Kezia Dunn. He fathered 10 children.

According to the 1820 U.S. Census, Hager was the head of a household of 30 people, including 10 slaves, in Woodford County, Kentucky. In that year the Hager family came to this area. He was a tinner by trade, though he purchased 80 acres of land in Flat Rock Township when he came here. As his financial resources increased, he added land until he was the owner of 1,000 acres, one of the most extensive land holders in this part of the state. He also owned a store in town for four years. Hager served as justice of the peace and was also judge of the county court for seven years.

He was deeply interested in church work. In the early days services were frequently held in his home.

He died on March 2, 1855, at the age of 74 in Bartholomew County and is buried at Liberty (also known as Hawpatch Liberty) Cemetery in Clifford.

### Abner and Betsy Mounts

When Abner Mounts was born in 1805 in Pennsylvania, his father, Abner Mounts, was 47 and his mother, Catharine Mumma, was 17. The family moved to Fairfield County, Ohio, where the elder Abner was convicted of killing his wife. Abner Sr. later broke out of prison.[2]

What happened to Abner Mounts Jr. between the time his father killed his mother and Jan. 11, 1824, when he married Elizabeth "Betsy" Rogers here, is unknown.

It's possible young Abner was taken in by relatives, who eventually moved here. Lending credence to that theory is the fact that Samuel Mounts and his son, Thomas, arrived here in 1821 from Scott County (and Kentucky prior to that), and some of the Mounts family members from western Pennsylvania moved to Ohio and Kentucky in the early 1800s.

Abner and Betsy were the parents of at least three sons. They both lived in the county until at least 1830, when they were listed on a U.S. Census report. Abner was living in Mahaska County, Iowa, in 1850 with sons, Roland and William, according to census records.

The father of First Presbyterian founder Abner Mounts, who went by the same name, was convicted of murdering his wife in Fairfield County, Ohio. This article, published in a Mississippi newspaper in 1813, appeared in papers around the nation.

### Edwin and Cynthia Brown

Edwin Brown Jr. was born Aug. 14, 1782, in Wilkes County, North Carolina, to Edwin Brown Sr. and Ruth Echols Brown. He married Cynthia McEwen (also born in 1782) on Sept. 29, 1811, in Wilkes County. The couple's son, Daniel McEwen Brown, was born in 1820 in Kentucky. By 1822, they had moved to Bartholomew County. Edwin died in 1827 here.

By 1840, Cynthia had moved to Fountain. She died in Fort Wayne.

### Samuel and Ruth Makinson

Samuel Makinson, the second elder of the church, served in that capacity until 1836, when he left for Iowa. He was listed in the 1820 Census as being a farmer in an unknown location in Delaware County (part of which later became known as Bartholomew). It is thought that Samuel and Ruth were both born in 1797 in Kentucky and were married in that state in 1817.

The couple's last name was spelled various ways in church histories over the years, including Mackinson, Miskimon and Miskimons.

### John Henry

John J. Henry purchased 160 acres of land here on Nov. 29, 1820. He married Virginia Redman in Bartholomew County on Nov. 28, 1839. No other information could be found regarding him.

### Martha Gabbert

Martha (Young) Gabbert was born on Sept. 18, 1791, in Lincoln County, Kentucky, to John Young Sr.

---
2 "Stop the Murderer!" *Natchez (Miss.) Gazette*, May 18, 1813.

and Mary "Polly" (Montgomery) Young. She married Jacob Gabbert, a native of Lexington, Virginia, in Kentucky in 1812, and the couple eventually moved to Flat Rock Township around 1820. They had eight children. Jacob, born in 1784, died in 1862, and Martha died in 1870. They are buried at Liberty Cemetery in Clifford.

**Andrew and Sarah Rogers**

Andrew Rogers was born in 1775 and died on Oct. 8, 1835. Sarah was born in 1780 and died less than two months after her husband, on Nov. 28, 1835. He bought 80 acres of land here on April 24, 1820, coming to Bartholomew County from Bethlehem, Indiana, on the Ohio River in Clark County. Their daughters, Jane and Mary Ann, were quite young when First Presbyterian came about. Andrew and Sarah are buried in the Rogers family cemetery in Petersville.

As for the three who joined a few days later:

**Maria (Stansbury) Wiles** was married to Akin A. Wiles at the time of chartering. She was born in 1797 in Essex County, New Jersey, and died on Dec. 28, 1882, in Bartholomew County. A Methodist and at one time trustee of that church in Columbus, A.A., as he was commonly known, was heavy-set and balding, "with a kindly heart and hospitable manner, which made him many warm friends." They were married in 1820 in Lebanon, Ohio, and moved to Columbus in 1822, bringing with them the first barrel of flour in Columbus. They built a hewed log house about 20 feet square where A.A. invited the first Methodist circuit rider to serve this county to preach. A potter by trade, A.A was treasurer of Bartholomew County from 1824 to 1825 and 1827 to 1829. He was also an overseer of the poor here before his death Feb. 11, 1845, at not quite 46 years old. The pair are buried in Columbus City Cemetery.

**Sarah F. Snyder** married Fred S. Snyder and had a daughter, Ruth, who died in 1892 and is buried in Columbus City Cemetery.

**Sarah Farmer**: No credible information could be found about her.

OTHER SOURCES:

Berkey, Carol. *First Presbyterian Church: A History*, 1999

"Joseph Hart and His Descendants." *The Republic*, Oct. 23, 1974.

History of Clinton County, Ohio: https://freepages.rootsweb.com/~henryhowesbook/genealogy/clinton.html

"Mounts Family Research Shared." *The Republic*, September 29, 1982.

Holmes, Maurice. *Court Records of Bartholomew County, 1822-1852*, 1977.

*History of Bartholomew County, 1888*. Published by Brant and Fuller, Chicago.

Slevin, Ruth M. *Bartholomew County Marriages, 1821-1850*. Copyright Walter R. Gooldy, 1985

Find a Grave Memorial page for David Hager: https://www.findagrave.com/memorial/11979645/david-hager

*Biographical Record of Bartholomew County Indiana, 1904*, B. F. Bowen Publisher.

*Original Tract book of Bartholomew County Indiana*, compiled by Jane F. Murphy. A bicentennial project of the Joseph Hart Chapter DNR, Columbus, 1976-77.

State of Pennsylvania U.S. Land Warrants

U.S. Census records

Bartholomew County Cemetery Records

Kentucky, Compiled Marriages, 1802-1850

US General Land office records

First Presbyterian Centennial Week program, 1924

# Our Early Days

**It was custom** in the early days of the congregation for church meetings to last four days, beginning on Fridays. If possible, the minister in charge would be assisted by other brethren in the ministry, or two ministers would share duties.

"Thus, for a series of years, most of the churches in these Western wilds were kept alive, and by God's blessings, made to grow," wrote Ninian S. Dickey.[1]

He added that these meetings, which consisted of prayer, singing and conversation, would draw people from as far as 50 miles away.

After a few years of meeting at the courthouse, citizens of all faiths banded together to form an organization called the "Columbus Liberty Meeting House and School House." The group raised money to purchase a lot on the north side of Tipton (now Third) Street east of Franklin and erected a building in 1831 that was then on the eastern edge of town to use as a schoolhouse and for religious meetings, regardless of denomination. It was called the "Classical Institute" by residents. Today, the Bartholomew County Historical Society building stands at the site.

It was the first church built in Columbus, and it was erected solely by volunteers. It "was about 50-by-25 feet, one story high, with a door in each end and the front," according to historian Williamson H. H. Terrell, who attended school there in 1833. "On either side of the door were two windows. In the center of the rear wall opposite the door was a pulpit. In front of it was the school master's desk. On either side of the pulpit were two windows corresponding to those in the front wall. The room was ceiled with boards and decorated with chewed wads of paper. It was heated by a large oblong stove."

A sketch of the Columbus Liberty Meeting House and School, where Presbyterians and Methodists worshipped starting in 1831. The building stood on Third (then Tipton) Street, east of Franklin Street.// Bartholomew County Historical Society

Both Presbyterians and Methodists had services there for some years. It was in this building that the Rev. Michael Remley, who was the supply minister for several Presbyterian churches in the area and made his home in Columbus, established the first Sabbath School, open to all children. This was the first example in a long history of advocacy for Christian education by the Columbus Presbyterian Church.

---

[1] *The Columbus Republican*, Jan. 7, 1875.

# 200 YEARS of FIRST PRESBYTERIAN CHURCH of COLUMBUS, INDIANA

## Ministers

M.A. REMLEY | Rev. BENJAMIN M. NYCE | Rev. N.S. DICKEY

Rev. G.S.J. BROWNE | Rev. ALEX PARKER | S.R. FRAZIER

F.W. FRASER | F.C. HOOD | Rev. C.G. RICHARDS

## Members who have entered the Ministry

Rev. CHARLES C. HART | W.T. HART | E.H. PENCE D.D.

GEO. B. PENCE | WALTER V. WALTMAN | ALEX. E. SHARP

Ministers during our early days included (from left):

Top row: Michael A. Remley, Benjamin M. Nyce, Ninian S. Dickey.
Row 2: George S. J. Browne, Alexander Parker, S. Robinson Frazier.
Row 3: Fenwick W. Fraser, Frank C. Hood, Charles Gorman Richards.

Members who had entered the ministry during our first 100 years:
Row 4: Charles C. Hart, William T. Hart, Edward Hart Pence.
Bottom row: George Billings Pence, Walter V. Waltman, Alexander Edward Sharp.

# 200 YEARS of FIRST PRESBYTERIAN CHURCH of COLUMBUS, INDIANA

The Methodists then built the first building in town used solely for worship. They had elected trustees 14 years earlier because Gen. John Tipton had promised them a 75-foot lot at the southeast corner of Washington and Fifth (then Harrison) streets.

But the general recanted on his promise, perhaps when he found out residents changed their minds about naming the city for him, and it wasn't until 1837 that the Methodists completed the title to the ground, subsequently erecting a building at a cost of $400. The Methodists graciously invited the Presbyterians to share the building.

\*\*\*

As the congregation grew, more than one elder served at a time.

Ninian S. Dickey, who served as minister from 1853 to 1870, listed the first 20 ruling elders in his memoirs printed in *The Columbus Republican* on Jan. 7, 1875. Joseph Hart was eventually joined by Samuel Makinson. Then came John Ritchey and Dr. Joseph A. Baxter.

Gideon Blackburn Hart, Joseph Hart's son who was instrumental in the formation of the Sand Hill branch of the church in 1847, was the fifth. He was followed by Samuel B. McKeehan.

### Elders

Judge DAVID HAGER — CHARTER MEMBER, FIRST TRUSTEE
Dr. WM. O. HOGUE
THOMAS HART
Dr. A.G. COLLIER
RANDOLPH GRIFFITH
JAMES R. HOFER
FREDRICK DONNER
ADAM KELLER
ANDREW H. GRAHAM
JOHN STOBO
JOHN SCOTT
JAMES B. SAFFORD
T. F. FITZGIBBON
JAMES LAUGHLIN

Some of our earliest elders, along with our first trustee, David Hager. Reprinted from the First Presbyterian Centennial program, 1924. Note that Frederick Donner's name was misspelled.

John Hubbert, Lewis Copperfield, Nicholas Gilman and Herman Barber, rounding out the first 10.

The second 10 consisted of Dr. Homer T. Hinman, Randolph Griffith, John Hofer, Thomas Hart (another of Joseph Hart's sons), Drs. W. O. Hogue and A.G. Collier, Andrew Graham, James Fisher, Boyd Donner and Frederick Donner.

*\*\*\**

In 1837, when conservatives took control of the General Assembly, four synods from New York and Ohio were expelled for their liberalism and cooperation with the Congregationalists. Individual congregations, including the Columbus Presbyterians, left to join the ousted group, forming the New School Presbyterian Church. Until reunion in 1870, the two groups remained separate entities. Liberalism of theological thought has been the byword of this congregation since its inception. Unfortunately, schisms within the Presbyterian Church have not been unknown since.

*\*\*\**

During the first few decades of its existence, the Presbyterian church here was served by various missionary ministers. The congregation didn't have anyone minister to them regularly until Remley did from 1832 to 1833 and didn't get its first installed minister until 1850, when James Brownlee was called as such.

Up to that time, John M. Dickey ministered here more than most. Among the group of ministers to supply Columbus during the first half of the 19th century, the Rev. Benjamin Nyce stood out. It was during his pastorate that the congregation built its first church building, on the southwest corner of Tipton (now Third) and Franklin streets, next to where the Crump Theatre stands today. It was due to Nyce's leadership and ability that this was possible.

"With his hammer and saw he (Nyce) made a full hand in the work, and by his energy and enthusiasm enlisted the sympathy and assistance of many who might not otherwise have been interested."

The lot, number 15 in the town's original plat, was purchased from partners John Young and John M. Gwin. The deed for moiety of Young bears the date July 27, 1846, but due to Gwin's business failure, the title was not completed for six years at a cost of $235.

Having purchased the land, the congregation still needed to erect a building, which proved difficult as the church "was feeble in members and munitions and felt itself too poor to undertake or even consider the building of a house of worship at that time."

Nyce, however, instituted an installment plan and aided by a few women, solicited subscriptions in money, work, building materials and anything else he could get. He began to erect the building and continued until supplies were exhausted. He then renewed his efforts in the same manner until work came to a standstill again. On one occasion, a local doctor donated a load of lumber he'd accepted as payment for services to a man who owned a sawmill if only the doctor would come to get it. The doctor passed the offer on to Nyce, who "engaged the largest team and wagon he could find and thriftily

---

> Having purchased the land, the congregation still needed to erect a building, which proved difficult as the church "was feeble in members and munitions and felt itself too poor to undertake or even consider the building of a house of worship at that time."

loaded" as much lumber as the team could carry to the building site.

This process continued until at last, the building was completed at a cost of $1,200. It was said that at least one virtue of having done it this way was that when the building was completed, the church owed no debt.

When finished, the building was said to be a substantial frame with a high foundation. It was roughly 60 feet long north to south and 50 feet wide. The audience room, as it was called, was "high-storied and had a splendid acoustic quality."

There were two entrances of double-wide doors on the north side, along with a belfry and choir platform. The pulpit was on the south side. Two aisles separated the benches used for seating, and a railing ran along the center line across the middle tier. The pews could accommodate up to 700 people. Both the east and west walls featured three large windows, and the room was heated by four large, wood-burning, oblong stoves. The lot was surrounded by a stout, wooden fence, with a double-wide gate at the Tipton (Third) Street entrance.

The congregation worshipped in this building for nearly 30 years, growing in numbers and extending its influence in good causes.

At one notable meeting, there was a meeting of the churches in the city to organize a women's crusade against saloons, early in the development of that movement. At the close of the meeting, the crusaders went from church to church, under the leadership of the ministers, and then began their campaign with a prayer meeting on the sidewalk in front of the most notorious saloon on Washington Street. Its name was not given.

The movement didn't immediately bear fruit but led later to the formation of the Woman's Christian Temperance Union, which was influential in enacting the 18th Amendment prohibiting the sale and transportation of beer and spirits in the United States. The amendment was popularly known as "Prohibition."

A sketch of our first building, located at the southwest corner of Tipton (now Third) and Franklin streets, next to where the Crump Theatre stands today. The building was completed in 1846 at a cost of $1,200. // Bartholomew County Historical Society.

The Presbyterians stayed in the building until the current church was built in 1874 to 1875. Their first building was sold for $3,000 to W.B. Whitney and was converted to retail space.

In addition to the Columbus church, Nyce built church buildings and congregations in Franklin,

Lowell Hill and Sugar Creek. The church he built for the Union Society in what was then Union Township was used by congregations of Presbyterians and German Lutherans. Nyce had Sunday school and worship services in English; the Lutheran services were in German. Although that building burned, the church still exists as St. John's Lutheran on Mauxferry Road.

Nyce was not only a builder of churches but also a teacher (he taught at the Columbus Academy, precursor to Columbus High School, and the Hartsville Seminary) and an inventor. He patented an insulated icehouse and developed systems of mechanical ice making and refrigeration without ice. Some of his concepts are still in use today.

The Rev. John M. Dickey is quoted as saying of Benjamin Nyce, "Modest, unassuming and eccentric with a lack of polish, the world never did him full justice. And when he died, a few short sentences in a single newspaper of the church were all that was allowed to tell of one of its brightest ornaments."

Among the others to minister to the fledgling congregation in its first 25 years of existence were:

- **James H. Johnston,** a native of New York who was licensed to preach in 1823 and moved to Marion, Indiana, the next year. One of the original trustees of Hanover College, he also was pastor of Centre Church in Crawfordsville (1843-1851, 1866-1867), principal of Crawfordsville Female Seminary (1851-1854), worked in missionary service in Montgomery County (1854-1866) and authored several books.

- **Samuel Gregg** was also an original trustee of Hanover College and was a pastor at First Presbyterian Church in Shelbyville for a time.

- **John F. Crowe,** credited with founding Hanover College, was born in Green County, Tennessee, which was then a part of North Carolina. He attended Transylvania University and Princeton Theological Seminary and was ordained a Presbyterian minister in 1815. After serving as pastor of two rural churches in Kentucky for several years, Crowe left Kentucky, apparently because of his unpopular abolitionist and pro-temperance views and became pastor of Hanover Presbyterian Church in 1823. In 1827, the Madison Presbytery asked Crowe to become the instructor and principal of the academy that it sought to found to train youths for the ministry. When Hanover Academy received its new charter as Hanover College in 1833, Crowe became vice president of the college. He guided Hanover College until 1859, the year before his death.

- **Eliphalet Kent,** of Puritan ancestry, was among the early pioneers of Shelbyville. He was the pastor at the Presbyterian church at Greenwood for four years before returning to Shelbyville and taking charge of the County Seminary.

- **Hillary Patrick** came to Indiana from Tennessee and appears to have been one of four Presbyterian missionaries who organized the First Presbyterian Church of Columbus, Mississippi, in 1829.

- **Michael Alexander Remley,** who was born in Virginia, was living in Jennings County by 1860.

> "Modest, unassuming and eccentric with a lack of polish, the world never did him (the Rev. Benjamin M. Nyce) full justice. And when he died, a few short sentences in a single newspaper of the church were all that was allowed to tell of one of its brightest ornaments."
>
> John M. Dickey

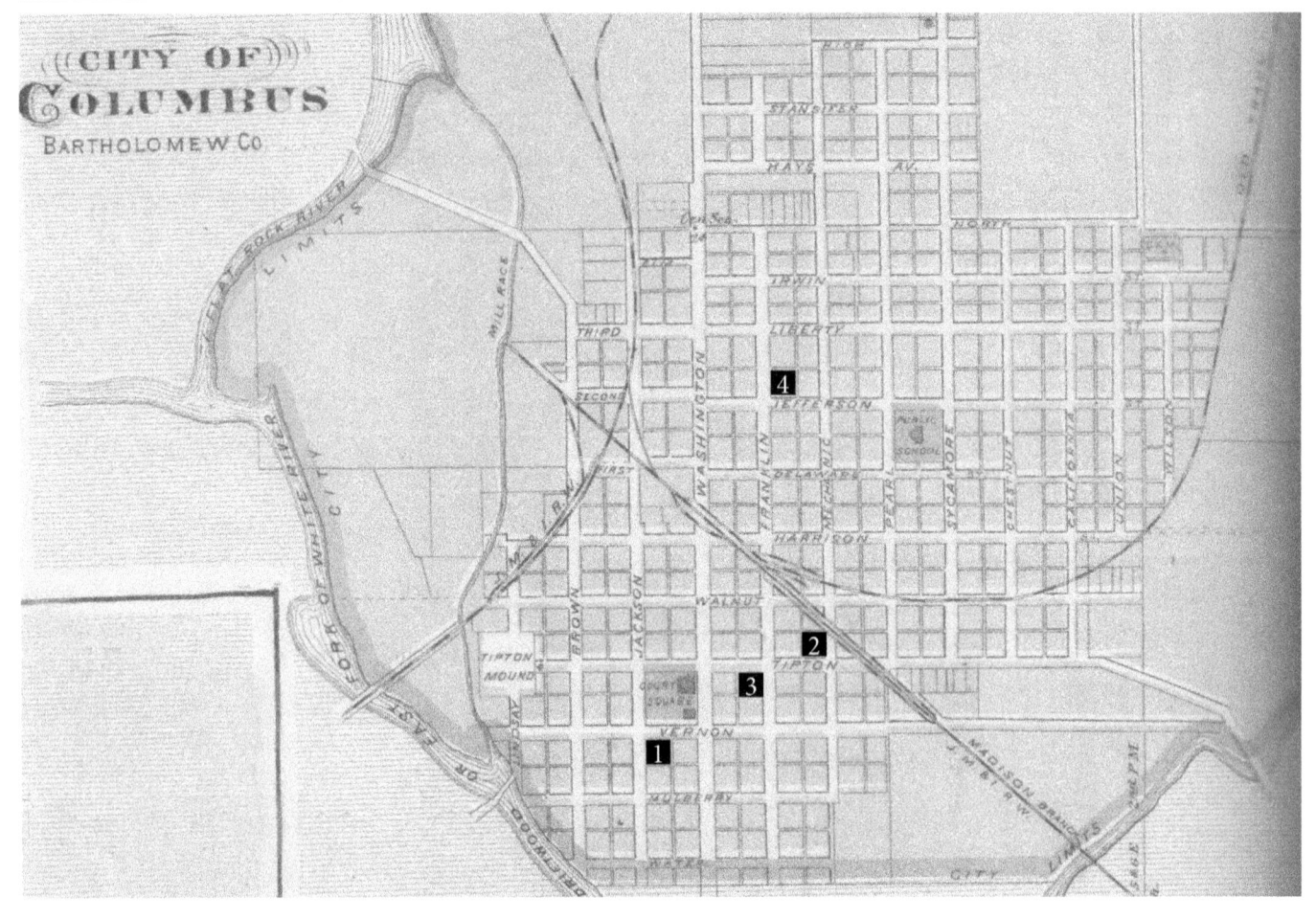

# 200 YEARS of FIRST PRESBYTERIAN CHURCH of COLUMBUS, INDIANA

A map of Columbus from 1876. // Bartholomew County Historical Society.
1 - Location of Hinkson's tavern, where local Presbyterians first met with a minister.
2 - Location of the Columbus Liberty Meeting House and School, where Presbyterians and Methodists both worshipped starting in 1831.
3 - Location of First Presbyterian's first church, used from 1846-1874.
4 - Location of the present-day church building,

He died in Rock Island County, Illinois, in 1887 and is buried in Hillcrest Cemetery in North Vernon.

- **Henry Little** was born in New Hampshire and graduated from Dartmouth College and Andover Theological Seminary. He was pastor for a short time of the Presbyterian Church in Oxford, Ohio, before being called to be superintendent of home missionaries in Indiana, a job he held until his death, except for two years when he served as pastor of Second Presbyterian Church in New Albany.

- **David Monfort** was born in Adams County, Pennsylvania, was educated at Transylvania University, in Lexington, Kentucky, and graduated from the theological seminary at Princeton, New Jersey. He spent the rest of his life as a preacher, supplying churches in Bethel; Terre Haute; Knightstown; Macomb, Illinois; Wilmington, Ohio; and Franklin, where he served for 20 years.

- **Joseph G. Monfort** lived in Greensburg until he became the principal of Glendale Female College in Glendale, Ohio, and worked at the Herald & Presbyter in Cincinnati.

- **Windsor A. Smith,** Henry Little's brother-in-law, first came here in 1837 and served off and on for 2½ years. He was the first pastor at the Presbyterian church in Aurora. He simultaneously served a congregation in Lawrenceburg. He also pastored a congregation in Brownstown.

- **Charles Merwin**, a Connecticut native, attended Auburn Theological Seminary in New York. He served as the pastor of Presbyterian congregations in New York, Ohio and Iowa, did some mission work and preached at other churches.

- **Others mentioned:** W.W. Wood, William Stimson, James Galliher, Daniel Latimore, S.M. Linton, Dr. Hinman, Thomas Hays.

\*\*\*

In 1850, the congregation, now almost 200 strong, called its first installed pastor, the Rev. James Brownlee, who had also served as pastor of the Presbyterian churches in Brownstown and Leavenworth before coming here. Though little is known of his time here, one interesting note regarding Brownlee was that in 1889, his analysis of congregational generosity was listed in The Indianapolis News. According to his calculations, the average annual contributions per head among various denominations were: Baptists, 36 cents; Methodists, 74 cents; Episcopalians, $1.37; Presbyterians, $3.17; and the Dutch, $3.21.

\*\*\*

Brownlee was succeeded by the Rev. Ninian Steele Dickey, son of the founding minister John M. Dickey, and Ninian served from 1853 to 1870. This was the first of many long pastorates that have been the hallmark of the Columbus Presbyterian Church.

Harriet Beecher Stowe, author of *Uncle Tom's Cabin*, was a good friend of Ninian S. Dickey.

Ninian Dickey, a close friend of author Harriet Beecher Stowe, went on to become one of the oldest Presbyterian ministers in the state. He was born in 1823 in New Washington, graduated from Wabash College in 1848 and studied theology at Lane Seminary in Cincinnati before immediately going into the ministry. He succeeded his father as minister in New Washington before coming to Columbus.

In a speech Dickey gave the day following the dedication of the current building in 1875 and reprinted in the Jan. 7, 1875, edition of The Columbus Republican, he recalled that the first time he saw Columbus was in 1843, when he passed through on his way from his father's home near Madison to Crawfordsville to study at Wabash College. Initially, he viewed Columbus as a small, unattractive city. But each time he passed through after that, he noted improvements.[2]

After leaving this area, he took over the ministry at a Presbyterian church in Mattoon, Illinois. His work took him to other churches in Illinois and Kansas and in Danville and Indianapolis, Indiana.[3]

---

2  *The Columbus Republican*, January 7, 1875.
3  "Rev. N. S. Dickey dead." *The Indianapolis Journal*, March 23, 1895.

In his second and final year at seminary he lived with the Stowe family. Harriet Beecher Stowe, one of the chief instructors at the school, penned the book, *Uncle Tom's Cabin*. Published in 1852, the novel had a profound effect on attitudes toward African Americans and slavery in the U.S. and is said to have "helped lay the groundwork for the Civil War."[4]

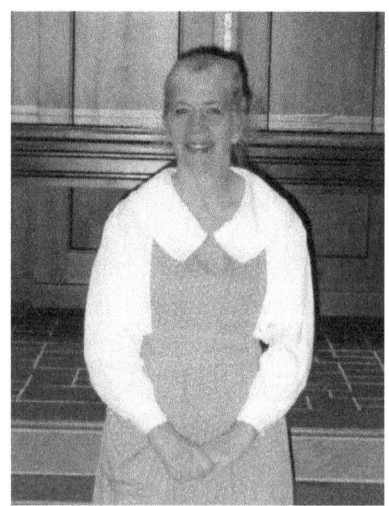

Stowe's affection for Dickey was said to be so great by the time he finished seminary that he was not permitted to leave the household without a keepsake, and she sent him home to Indiana with a small heating stove. "For years afterward, it was his delight to point out the relic as an important feature in the literary work of Harriet Beecher Stowe and the stove by which the author sat while she wrote *Uncle Tom's Cabin*."[5]

Shortly after seminary, he married Jane Davis. They had three sons and two daughters.

In its story announcing Dickey's death in 1895 after 43 years in the pulpit, *The Indianapolis Journal* said of him: "Mr. Dickey was a man possessed of wonderful courage and the strongest convictions." A few weeks prior to that, the 72-year-old Dickey had undergone an operation to amputate a tuberculosis-infected leg at City Hospital in Indianapolis. He had been rapidly recovering and was thought to be days away from returning to his home in that city. But he soon became nauseous and began hemorrhaging and having other subsequent attacks that could not be stopped. Doctors thought that the hemorrhage started from a tubercular deposit in one of Dickey's lungs.[6]

Left: Member Rich Eynon portrayed Ninian S. Dickey as part of the 175th anniversary festivities during services on Jan. 10, 1999. Right: Beth Newman portrayed charter member Mary Hart during services on Dec. 27, 1998.

"Mr. Dickey was a man possessed of wonderful courage and the strongest convictions."

The Indianapolis Business Journal on Ninian S. Dickey

OTHER SOURCES:
Berkey, Carol. *First Presbyterian Church: A History*, 1999.
First Presbyterian Centennial Week program, 1924
James H. Johnston papers, February 16, 1833
Discover Indiana: Second Presbyterian Church/Second Baptist Church
*The Cyclopedia of Biblical, Theological, and Ecclesiastical Literature*, edited by John McClintock and James Strong.
Hubbard, Rev. Dr. Joseph W. *The History of the Presbyterian Church in Iowa 1837-1900*, Presbyterian Church in the U.S.A. Synod of Iowa, 1907.
*The Columbus Republican*, Jan. 7, 1875.
*History of Shelby County, Indiana*, Chadwick 1909.

---

4 Kaufman, Will. *The Civil War in American Culture*. Edinburgh University Press, 2006.
5 "Rev. N. S. Dickey dead." *The Indianapolis Journal*, March 23, 1895.
6 Ibid.

# Constructing Our Current Building

**The Rev. Ninian S. Dickey** was followed as First Presbyterian minister in Columbus by Alexander Parker, a tireless worker who became widely known in the community and the church. This was unusual at a time as congregations tended to be clannish. Parker was much loved and remained pastor for 13 years.

He was born in Georgetown, Ohio, in 1829 and started school at Marietta College before dropping out due to health reasons. He graduated from Lane Seminary in Cincinnati and was ordained in 1858. He served churches in Allensville, Jacksonville, North Madison and Connersville, Indiana, before coming to Columbus in 1870.

Eventually he moved to Orange, California, remaining there until he retired with more than 50 years of ministry to his credit. During his tenure at Orange, the congregation grew five-fold. He served as moderator of the California Presbyterian Senate in 1899 and was a member of the General Assembly six times. He also received an honorary degree from Hanover College, an institution he had served as a trustee for more than 10 years.[1] He died in 1910 in his Ohio hometown.

Following his departure, the nondenominational Parker Croquet Club, named for the

The newly constructed building, just after the sanctuary was dedicated in 1885.

---
[1] "Rev. Parker rounds out a half century." *The Evening Republican*, July 9, 1907.

# 200 YEARS of FIRST PRESBYTERIAN CHURCH of COLUMBUS, INDIANA

preacher, continued to flourish at the rear of the residence of Dr. W.O. Hogue at the southwest corner of Sixth and Franklin streets for some time.[2]

\*\*\*

It was during Parker's tenure here that the congregation erected the building in which it remains to this day.

The congregation had been determined to build a new and bigger building and in 1871 purchased land for that purpose at the corner of Seventh and Franklin (then Jefferson) streets. An architect from Hope, Levi L. Levering, was hired to design the new church. The contract to erect the church was given to Kellar & Brockman and was completed at a cost of $26,000 (roughly $800,000 in today's money).[3]

Construction began in 1874, and on July 8, nearly 50 years to the day after the church was chartered, the cornerstone was laid, with Parker preaching on the text, "What mean ye by these stones." By the end of the year, the roof was on, the lecture room was complete and the steeple framework in place. Eventually, a large, 2-ton brass bell was placed in the steeple. It is still rung before every service today.

Early financial contributors to the effort were Elder Randolph Griffith, who gave $2,500, and Brainard Whitney, who donated $3,000 despite having no connection to the church. Others gave according to their means, and it looked like it would only be a few months before the entire project was paid for.

The congregation's farewell service in the old church was conducted on Sunday, Dec. 27, 1874, and on the following Sunday, Jan. 3, 1875, a dedicatory service was conducted in the new lecture room, the sanctuary not being ready yet for worship.

---

2  John Scott memoirs, 1974
3  *History of Bartholomew County, Indiana, 1888* (Bartholomew County Historical Society)

## Lecture Room dedication

On Sunday last, the lecture room of the new edifice of the Presbyterian church was dedicated to the service of God. The church proper not yet being completed, and the congregation being without a place in which to meet, it became a necessity that a portion of the building be prepared for occupancy and consecrated to worship; hence the energy of the society has been directed towards furnishing, carpeting and seating that portion while work has been partly discontinued on the others.

It is probably a fitting time for *The Democrat* to give publicity to the financial affairs of the society in reference to this edifice and to appeal to a generous public without regard to religious views for aid to complete this noble edifice. At the start it was intended by the trustees of the church to expend about $15,000 in the construction of the proposed edifice, and preparations were made to meet such an outlay.

A plan was presented which was approved, the cost being about $15,000, and work was commenced. It was found however, that the estimated cost, as is not unusual in buildings of this nature, would fall far short of the real cost, but as great outlays had been made and contracts entered into, to retrace the steps taken would be ruinous, and the trustees felt they could do nothing but advance, but they knew it was an advance in face of great difficulties.

*The (Columbus) Democrat*
Jan. 8, 1875

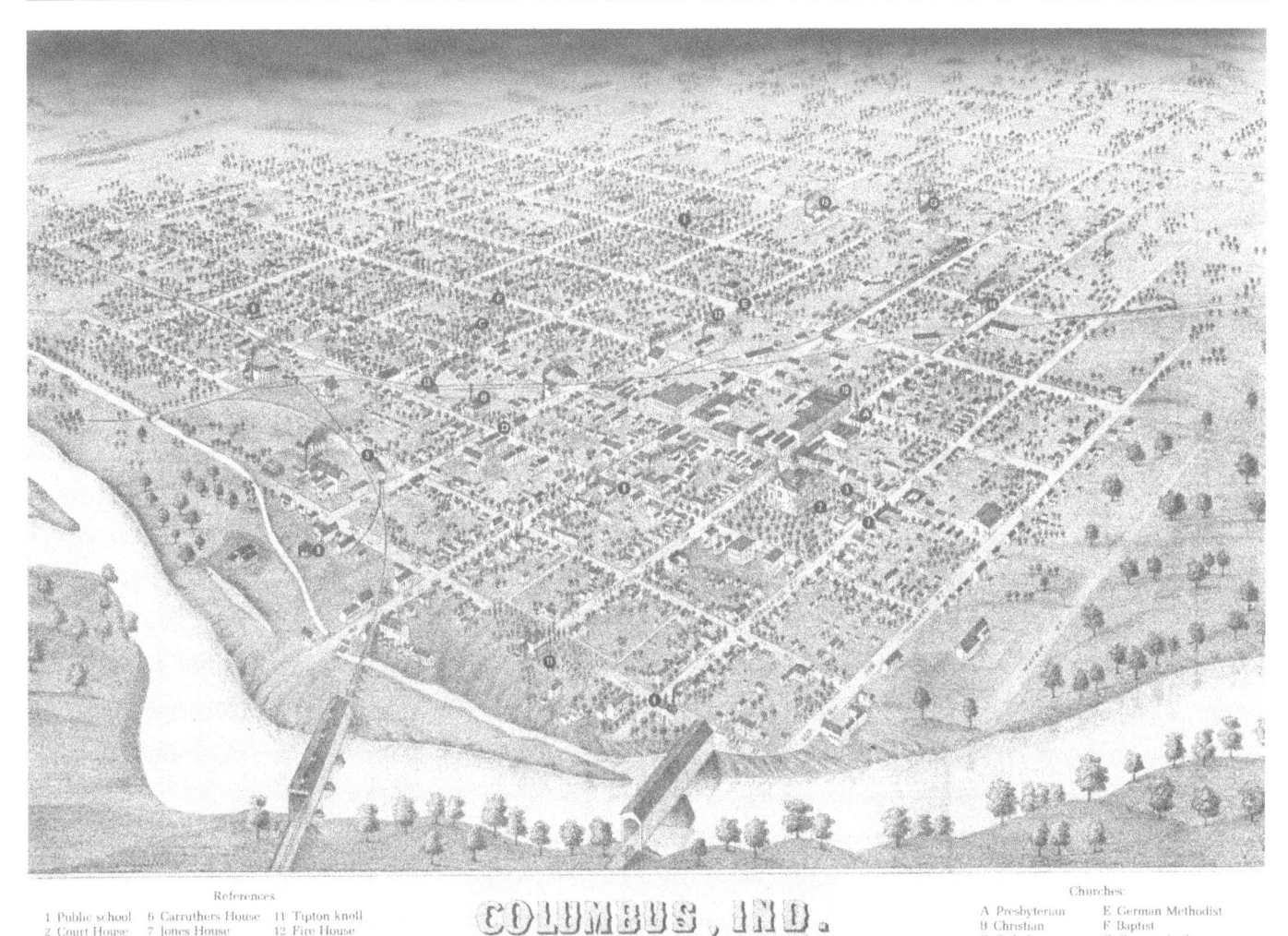

# 200 YEARS of FIRST PRESBYTERIAN CHURCH of COLUMBUS, INDIANA

**References**

1 Public school
2 Court House
3 Jail
4 Water works
5 J.M.I. depot
6 Carruthers House
7 Jones House
8 Jackson House
9 Gas works
10 McEwen bank
11 Tipton knoll
12 Fire House
13 Hege-Mathes Lumber
14 Keller-Brockman Lumber
15 Brinkley Furniture

**COLUMBUS, IND.**

Bird's-eye view of Columbus in 1871

**Churches:**

A Presbyterian
B Christian
C Catholic
D Methodist
E German Methodist
F Baptist
G German Lutheran

Bartholomew County Historical Society

"The Lecture room of the new Presbyterian church was crowded with ladies and gentlemen at an early hour to witness the dedicatory ceremonies," *The Columbus Republican* reported in its Jan. 7, 1875, edition. "The room was comfortably warm, and everyone seemed to sit easy in the new chairs."

On the west side of the room hung a crayon picture of the first church ever erected in this city, over which was inscribed in large letters, "For who shall despise the day of small things. – Zachariah 15:10" and beneath it was "1824."

On the west side of the pulpit hung a picture of the previous church on Tipton Street, above which read, "Lord, I have loved the habitation of thy house." Behind the desk was a large banner bearing the words, "A jubilee shall that fiftieth be unto you. – Leviticus 25:11." A drawing of the new church was also hung in the lecture room, and upon it was inscribed in large, German characters, "The Lord is in his holy temple."

Ministers present for the dedication were the Rev. Alexander Parker, the present pastor; Dr. Heckman, president of Hanover College; Dr. Little of Madison;

31

# 200 YEARS of FIRST PRESBYTERIAN CHURCH of COLUMBUS, INDIANA

Father Kent of Shelbyville; Father Remley of Edinburg; and Rev. N. S. Dickey, former pastor of the church, now of Greenville, Illinois.

Parker announced the program for the morning and evening services. After singing and prayer, Heckman delivered the dedicatory sermon and also delivered a sermon that evening. On Monday, Dickey delivered a historical sketch of the church, which was printed in its entirety in *The Columbus Republican* the following Thursday.

But what had started with such promise was soon in peril.

Shortly before the dedication, the death of Griffith, an ardent supporter of the new building who had been expected to make another large contribution toward the construction costs, was a severe blow, though one the congregation believed it could overcome, and work continued.

Almost immediately, another blow fell. Whitney, another expected large contributor, was forced to declare bankruptcy. He was president of Farmers' Bank and owner of one of the city's largest industries. The closing of his pork packing operation brought hardship and depression to the whole community.

Within weeks of that disaster, Trustee Thomas Hays died suddenly. He, too, had indicated that he would make a large gift to the building. Within a few short months, all the expected large donations had evaporated.

> The congregation was in a state of shock. Serious consideration was given to selling the uncompleted building. In the end, it was decided to stop all construction for the time being, continue worship in the lecture room and try to raise the money necessary to complete the work.

> The congregation was in a state of shock. Serious consideration was given to selling the uncompleted building. In the end, it was decided to stop all construction for the time being, continue worship in the lecture room and try to raise the money necessary to complete the work.

The congregation was in a state of shock. Serious consideration was given to selling the uncompleted building. In the end, it was decided to stop all construction for the time being, continue worship in the lecture room and try to raise the money necessary to complete the work.

Once again, the women of the church raised money through many projects. They had strawberry and ice cream socials, served dinners and gave concerts, readings, lectures and cantatas, with all proceeds going toward the completion of the sanctuary. A Sunday school group of women called the Dorcas Band earned money to buy the iron fence that still borders some of the church property.

It took a long time, a lot of effort and the support of the entire community, but at last the work was completed. Francis J. Crump and Christian Martin donated the cost of plastering. The family of Randolph Griffith gave the rose window on the west wall as a memorial to him, and the family of Thomas Hays gave the middle window on the south wall in his memory. The Light Brigade, a philanthropic organization with the church through the late 1800s, gave the gas chandeliers. New pulpit furniture and pews were purchased. Fred Dahn made possible the sidewalks and grading of the yard, and the Dorcas Band gave the wrought iron fence.

One gift in particular seems to have enabled the completion of the work, and that came from Thomas Gaff. He had no ties with the church and only business ties with Columbus.

His home was in Aurora. But he had seen the determination and dedication of the church members and wanted to help. His gift secured the promise of a matching gift from the Presbyterian Board of Church Erection.

Finally, the new sanctuary was dedicated on May 31, 1885. "DEDICATED: After Twelve Years of Discouragements" trumpeted *The Evening Republican* in its pages the following day. The sanctuary and lecture room were overfilled as the two aisles in the sanctuary (there were three sections of pews in those days instead of the two we have today) were crowded with additional chairs.

"Both rooms were handsomely and lavishly decorated with flowers," the story reported.

Parker, who had been replaced as pastor by George S. J. Browne by this time, returned to give the dedicatory sermon. Dickey was also in attendance. Bates performed the duties of organist. The choir opened the festivities in song, the Rev. R. D. Black provided the invocation and elder Sweeney made the scripture reading. Following more singing, elder Harper led the congregation in prayer. Browne "then began a very able sermon in which he recounted the difficulties, the struggles, the discouragements passed through that they might meet together on the present occasion."

Other churches in town canceled their services that morning, so that all could attend. Black, of the Methodist Church, and the Rev. Z.T. Sweeney, of Tabernacle Christian, took part in the service. Afterward, Black announced that nearly $1,000 was still to be paid, and those attending the services pledged nearly the entire amount.

Browne and Crump led off with donations of $50 each, and within a few minutes $625 was added. It wasn't long before the entire $1,000 had been raised.

> ## Sanctuary dedication program
>
> Program of the dedication services at the Presbyterian church tomorrow at 10 a.m.:
>
> Singing of Doxology, audience
> Invocation, the Rev. R.D. Black
> Anthem, choir
> Scripture reading, the Rev. Z.T. Sweeney
> Hymn 20, "Arise, O King of Grace, Arise," audience
> Prayer, the Rev. N. Harper
> Hymn 339, "All Hail the Power of Jesus Name," audience
> Announcements
> Presentation of church for dedication, the Rev. Geo. S.J. Browne
> Sermon, the Rev. Alex. Parker
> Appropriate remarks to the occasion, the Rev. Black and others
> Dedication prayer, the Rev. N.S. Dickey
> Dedication hymn 1016, audience
> Benediction, Pastor Geo. S.J. Browne
>
> The Republican
> May 30, 1885

# 200 YEARS of FIRST PRESBYTERIAN CHURCH of COLUMBUS, INDIANA

The efforts to complete the church and pay off all its debt over the course of more than a decade made quite an impression upon the community.

"The foundation stones of that magnificent edifice whose spire pointing heavenward is destined to wield a silent influence for cycles to come that will tell in eternity, were laid under the brightest prospects," *The Evening Republican* stated. The time and effort it took to complete the project seemed "to test to the uttermost the faith, the energy, the strength of character, the willingness of purpose of His people to do something for Him, for themselves, for society, and for the generations unborn who will gather within its walls and be made better, purer, holier by the influences there exerted."[4]

*The History of Bartholomew County*, published in 1888, described the building as "a magnificent brick edifice, of modern style of architecture, and is divided into five apartments, viz.: auditorium, lecture room, infant class room, Bible class room and study." The small classrooms were on the north side of the lecture room, and the study was in the bell tower. Membership at the time was around 270.

The building has undergone several expansions and renovations over the years but is still in use today.

---

4   *The Evening Republican*, June 1, 1885.

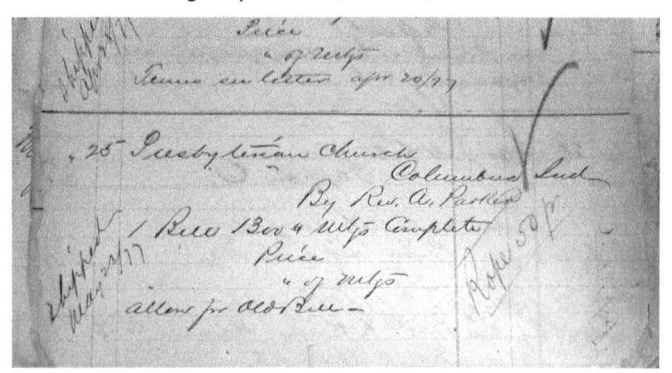

Clockwise from top: The 2-ton brass bell situated in the steeple was cast in 1877 by McShane Bell Foundry of Baltimore, Maryland. Founded in 1856, McShane is America's oldest church bell company. The bill of sale for the bell, showing the bell was shipped on "May 23/77" (lower left). According to a representative from McShane, the bell was ordered on April 25 of that year. No purchase price is listed, but bells were sold for about 19-22 cents per pound for the bell and about 50 cents per pound for all the hardware, according to McShane. // Zack Ellison

# 200 YEARS of FIRST PRESBYTERIAN CHURCH of COLUMBUS, INDIANA

# A Parade of Pastors

**Beginning in 1884**, First United Presbyterian Church, as it was then called, had several pastors staying five years or less:

- **George S. J. Browne** (1884-1886), the pastor when the current building's sanctuary was dedicated, left the following year to pastor a church in Bowling Green, Ohio. Originally from Cincinnati, Browne was instrumental in the building of many Presbyterian churches and spent five years doing mission work in Chicago. His wife was Emma Carpenter, and they had four daughters and one son.[1] Well-liked, he once returned from a trip to Cincinnati to find the women of our church had added a "very handsome table and an elegant chair" to his study.[2] During his two years in Columbus, he established a chapter of The Young People's Society of Christian Endeavor here.[3]

- **Samuel Robinson (S. R.) Frazier** (1887-1891) was also well-liked and admired, and it was said much good resulted in the church and community due to his service here. His farewell sermon, delivered on Nov. 15, 1891, was reported to be "a very impressive affair. To him, his friends, and his congregation, it was also a sad affair." In his final address to his congregation, Frazier admonished the members "to push it forward. To maintain the present high standing religiously and socially, and to ever look upward and advance."[4] He was given a gold-headed cane as a going-away gift at a reception two nights later by the 40 members of the Grand Army of the Republic (a fraternal organization of Union veterans of the Civil War) in attendance. An Ohio native, he spent time in the ministry with the Union Army during the Civil War and was with Gen. William T. Sherman on the march from Atlanta to the Atlantic Ocean. He died in 1914 following a pastorate at Tabernacle Presbyterian Church in Youngstown, Ohio.[5]

- **Fenwick Williams Fraser** (1892-1896), born in Nova Scotia, was in his mid-20s and single when he took the pulpit at First Presbyterian. While pastor here, a "bitter and singular personal quarrel"

> In his final address to his congregation, (Samuel Robinson) Frazier admonished the members "to push it forward. To maintain the present high standing religiously and socially, and to ever look upward and advance."
>
> The Evening Republican

---

1 Goss, Rev. Charles Frederic. *Cincinnati: The Queen City: 1788-1912, Vol. III Biographical.* The S. J. Clarke Publishing Co., 1912.
2 *The Evening Republican*, May 16, 1885.
3 John Scott memoirs, 1974.
4 *The Evening Republican*, November 16, 1891.
5 Giffin Genealogic Family History, Central Publishing House, Cleveland, Ohio, 1927

# 200 YEARS of FIRST PRESBYTERIAN CHURCH of COLUMBUS, INDIANA

A view of downtown Columbus looking northeast from the county courthouse tower in late 1891. At left is Washington Street. First Presbyterian is in the black oval at top. // Bartholomew County Historical Society

was said to have developed between him and Z. T. Sweeney of Tabernacle Christian Church, although they once had been close friends. In 1894, Fraser married Bertha C. Cooper, sister of Kent Cooper who went on to become the executive director of the Associated Press, and the daughter of George W. Cooper, who was mayor of Columbus before serving in the U.S. Congress from 1889 to 1895. One of the wedding guests was Mary Emily Donelson Wilcox, grand-niece of President Andrew Jackson.[67] Wilcox erroneously claimed throughout her life to be the first child born at the White House; she was actually the second white child born there and most likely the ninth overall.[8] Fraser announced in March 1896 that he would be leaving, citing irreconcilable differences with the elders as to how the church should be governed. It was said, however, that the larger portion of the congregation would be sad to see him go, and as a sermonizer, he had few equals.[9] He gave his farewell sermon the following July.[10] He then pastored a church 40 miles south of Winnipeg, Manitoba, and eventually settled in Massillon, Ohio.

---

6  *The Evening Republican*, October 18, 1894.
7  *The Boonville (Indiana) Republican*, August 31, 1905.
8  https://www.grunge.com/1434835/every-baby-born-in-white-house/ November 1, 2023.
9  *The Evening Republican,* March 2, 1896.
10 *The Evening Republican,* July 17, 1897.

- **Frank C. Hood** (1896-1900). His pastorate started with the death of a member on the morning of his first sermon here. Julia Cook, who had expressed to her daughter a great desire to hear the new preacher, died as Hood entered the pulpit on the morning of Oct. 25, 1896. He conducted her funeral the next day.[11] He resigned in November 1900, taking a "tempting" offer from the Winona (Indiana) Assembly Educational Bureau to start a training school for boys it planned to organize. Coming to Columbus from Indianapolis, he was said to be "an earnest Christian gentleman and one who commanded respect from every class of people."[12] [13]

- **Charles Gorman Richards** (1901-1906), a native of Pittston, Pennsylvania, was a few days away from graduating from McCormick Theological Seminary in Chicago when he was unanimously elected to the pastorate here on April 25, 1901. He had been filling in since Hood's resignation quite admirably, "and with no effort at all he worked himself into the hearts of the entire congregation." A graduate of Princeton University, Richards "has already large experience in pulpit and pastoral work for a young man" when he came to Columbus.[14] He left for Sterling, Illinois, in July 1906 after a successful term here. While in Columbus, the church was "freed from debt and its properties enlarged and beautified. Its membership has very substantially grown in numbers, strength and influence." The congregation's positive influence had been increasingly felt in the community and with fellow churches. Richards had a keen sense of right and a devotion to the city. "With fearlessness, but with sound discretion and becoming modesty, also he exercised the delicate duties of citizenship to honor and credit of the church," according to a statement by members of session supplied to the local newspaper.[15]

> "With fearlessness, but with sound discretion and becoming modesty, also he (Charles Gorman Richards) exercised the delicate duties of citizenship to honor and credit of the church."
>
> The Session

- **Amos Kenton Mattingly** (1907-10). A native of Kentucky, Mattingly came to Columbus from Second Presbyterian Church in Madison, Indiana.[16] He went on to manage 12 Chautauqua adult education centers in Oklahoma in addition to overseeing the Chautauqua in Oklahoma City.[17] He led other churches before eventually settling in Arkansas, where he died in 1945 at the age of 70.

Distressingly, two of these pastors were dismissed by the congregation. Hood, though loved and respected, was so distracted by his wife's mental illness that he was no longer an effective pastor and was asked to seek another pulpit. Mattingly was asked to leave. Feelings were so acrimonious that his picture was not included in the 1924 Centennial Program 15 years later. Although an interim service by former pastor

---

11 *The Evening Republican,* Oct. 27, 1896.
12 *The Evening Republican,* Nov. 5, 1900.
13 *The Evening Republican,* Nov. 3, 1900.
14 *The Evening Republican,* April 26, 1901.
15 *The Evening Republican,* June 23, 1906.
16 *The Evening Republican,* Nov. 15, 1906.
17 *The Evening Republican,* May 9, 1910.

Alexander Parker had eased tensions somewhat, the Rev. Alexander Sharp, who came in 1910, still found the congregation in something of an uproar.

\*\*\*

But if ministers came and went, elders, once elected, served for life or until they moved from Columbus. In its first century, the church had only 43 men hold the office of elder. Joseph Hart served 17 years. Later elders served even longer terms, but the dean of them all was Frederick Donner, who served 49 years

\*\*\*

Perhaps the most important development to come from the period was the introduction of Grace Chapel, which underscored the emphasis the congregation had placed on Christian education since its founding. In 1898, spurred by a sermon by the Rev. Hood on the importance of Christian education, some of the women of the church, including Mary Donner, began an outreach program to the children living in a neglected neighborhood on the east side of the city. Not really knowing what the response might be, they opened a Sunday school in a donated storeroom on California Street and invited the children to come.

The program was so successful that on April 15, 1900, the church erected a small chapel at 905 N. Wilson St. (corner of Ninth and Wilson) to serve both the children and their parents. They eventually hired a ministerial student to serve the chapel congregation, but for many years the work was all volunteer. There was a house of prostitution in the area. Through the work of the Grace Chapel volunteers and the Rev. Alexander E. Sharp Sr., the madam of the house was converted to Christianity and carried on a ministry to many people in need.

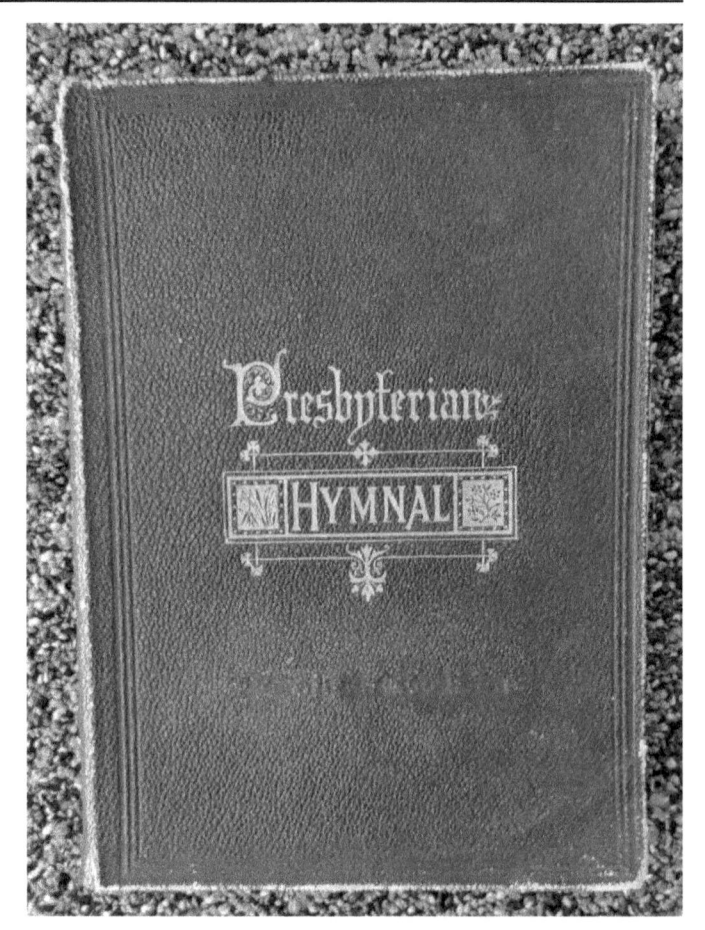

Presbyterians continued this mission for 24 years. In 1922, believing that the neighborhood would be better served by a neighborhood church, they sold the building to a Free Methodist congregation, which occupied it until 1948.[18] The building, which eventually became home to four apartments, was razed in 2014.[19]

---
18 *The Evening Republican,* March 19, 1960.
19 *The Republic,* Sept. 15, 2014.

# John Scott memories

John Scott, whose family moved next door to First United Presbyterian in 1882 when he was but a few months old, wrote in his memoirs that the "church has played an important part in my life ever since. It is a wonderful thing to be a part of this community."

His memories as a child growing up in the church, which were collected in connection with the 150th anniversary of the church in 1974, add a great deal of flavor to the congregation's history. Some of those memories were reproduced in the 175th anniversary book published in 1999. A selection of it is below:

> I am wondering what the new century will bring. Will the children find the elders austere and cold as I did? When my father was named an elder, I realized they were not so frightening after all. I think it was the beards and their advanced age (all over 50!) that made them a little scary.
>
> Our family attended services every Sunday morning and evening along with Sunday School and Christian Endeavor, and prayer services Wednesday evening. In the summertime, during Wednesday evening services, I could often hear other children playing in the street, which was a cause of some envy. Hymn singing shut out some of that tantalizing noise from outside. I have always liked church music.
>
> Speaking of music, one time when John Bonham was singing a solo, brother Walter and I spotted an owl over the choir loft. We began to laugh, much to the embarrassment of our mother, who tried to shush us. But soon everyone was laughing. Poor Mr. Bonham thought we were laughing at him, and he didn't return to church for six months.
>
> Mrs. Lawrence Ong was organist. I pumped the organ for her when she practiced. Her husband, a banker, was church treasurer and later an elder. Her brother, Prof. Andrew Graham, who was superintendent of the public schools as well as our Sunday School teacher, sang in the choir. I remember their families well, along with the Frederick Donners, because we sat in the fourth pew, and they sat in front of us.
>
> I remember with much happiness Sunday School picnics at Perry's Woods [now Donner Park] and Christmas exercises in the sanctuary. There was always a tall tree lighted with wax candles and Prof. Graham, with his grey beard, deep voice and jovial manner, was naturally equipped to be Santa Claus.
>
> I am grateful to this congregation not only for the fun times but even more for the loving nurture which I have received. It has blessed my life.

John Scott

# The E.R.O.

By the time we had become a little too strenuous for lady teachers, we were turned over to Dr. E. E. Edenburn, who could have managed four span of army mules. When the Rev. Charles Gorman Richards succeeded the Rev. Frank Hood, he wanted the boys class, but we still honored old Doc by calling our class the E.R.O, the Edenburn-Richards Organization.

— Excerpt from *I Discover Columbus* by Will Marsh

From left from the top: Pliny Pence, Pence Orr, Calvin Moore, Will Marsh, Harry Dehmer, Lawrence Orr, Ferd Cooper, Dave Pence, Clarence Webb, Edgar Abbott, Roland Williams, Herman Lederhaus

The Pences and the Orrs were descendants of Joseph Hart.

# 200 YEARS of FIRST PRESBYTERIAN CHURCH of COLUMBUS, INDIANA

The sanctuary in our centennial year, 1924.

Seal adopted in 1892

Seal adopted in 1959

PRESBYTERIAN CHURCH (USA)

Seal adopted in 1985

# The Alexander Sharp Sr. Era

**When the Rev. Alexander Sharp Sr.** came to Columbus from Ohio in November 1910, he brought with him wide experience. In addition to his pastoral work, which had endeared him to his flock in Ohio, he and his wife, Alethea, had been missionaries in Colombia, and he had been associated with the Dwight L. Moody and John McNeill evangelistic work in Chicago. A native of Liverpool, England, Sharp had come to the United States at the age of 18 in 1890 after attending revival services conducted by Moody. After two years at the Moody Bible Institute, he earned degrees from Centre College in Danville, Kentucky, and McCormick Seminary in Chicago.

Alexander E. Sharp Sr.

Sharp, a 6-foot-tall, solidly but compactly built man with a distinctly British accent, had preached in Columbus a few months prior to his arrival as full-time pastor, and he made a most favorable impression upon the congregation during those appearances.[1]

A biography of the man in an encyclopedia of Presbyterianism said: "Of a clear well-balanced judgment, and excellent powers of analysis, he has great patience and steadiness of will. His friends are attracted by a conspicuous modesty and charity."[2]

Ross Crump, historian and lifelong member of the congregation, wrote of his childhood memories of Sharp: "His accent was different from the Midwestern accents we were used to. He was a gentle man, a delightful personality and a dedicated Christian. I remember really listening to his sermons, which is unusual for a young boy. For preaching, he always wore the usual garb of a Presbyterian minister, a cutaway morning coat with striped trousers."

\*\*\*

In Columbus, Sharp quickly became known for his work with young men, both through the YMCA and the Boy Scouts.

He helped organize the first Boy Scout troop in Columbus in 1913, serving as scoutmaster for Troop 1. Ten boys attended the first meeting at the Presbyterian church. The organization was open to boys of any faith.[3]

---

1 *The Evening Republican,* Sept. 12, 1910.
2 *Encyclopedia of the Presbyterian Church in the United States of America.* Presbyterian Encyclopedia Publishing Co., Philadelphia, Penn., 1884.
3 *The Evening Republican,* June 26, 1913.

The YMCA called Sharp to assist in its war work in 1918, and the church granted him a leave of absence of roughly eight months for that purpose. The YMCA of those days was a much different organization than it has evolved into today. Founded in 1903 as an industrial department, it gave assistance to railroad workers, miners, lumbermen and immigrants. During World War I, the YMCA supported U.S. soldiers.[4]

Sharp was called into the YMCA to be one of three men charged with running the branch at Camp Zachary Taylor, a military training camp at West Point, Kentucky, just southwest of Louisville overlooking the Ohio River. The camp had a base hospital and trained soldiers for overseas deployment. Sharp's duties as educational and religious secretary included providing recreational, educational and/or religious work with the service personnel.

At its peak in the summer of 1918, about 64,000 soldiers were stationed at Camp Taylor. One of the soldiers who trained there during Sharp's tenure was F. Scott Fitzgerald, who went on to become a world-renowned novelist. His book "The Great Gatsby" was inspired by his weekend forays into Louisville from the camp. He spent only one month at the camp, arriving in March 1918 as a lieutenant.[5]

\*\*\*

During Sharp's nearly 23 years of ministry in Columbus, the congregation faced the First World War, the rise of the Ku Klux Klan and the beginnings of the Great Depression, which hit Columbus hard. The Klan was strong in Columbus and Indiana in the 1920s, but only one Presbyterian was a Klansman, so the church was affected only peripherally. In Columbus, the Klan was more anti-Catholic than anti-Black, and it spread the rumor that Catholics had stored arms in the church basement.

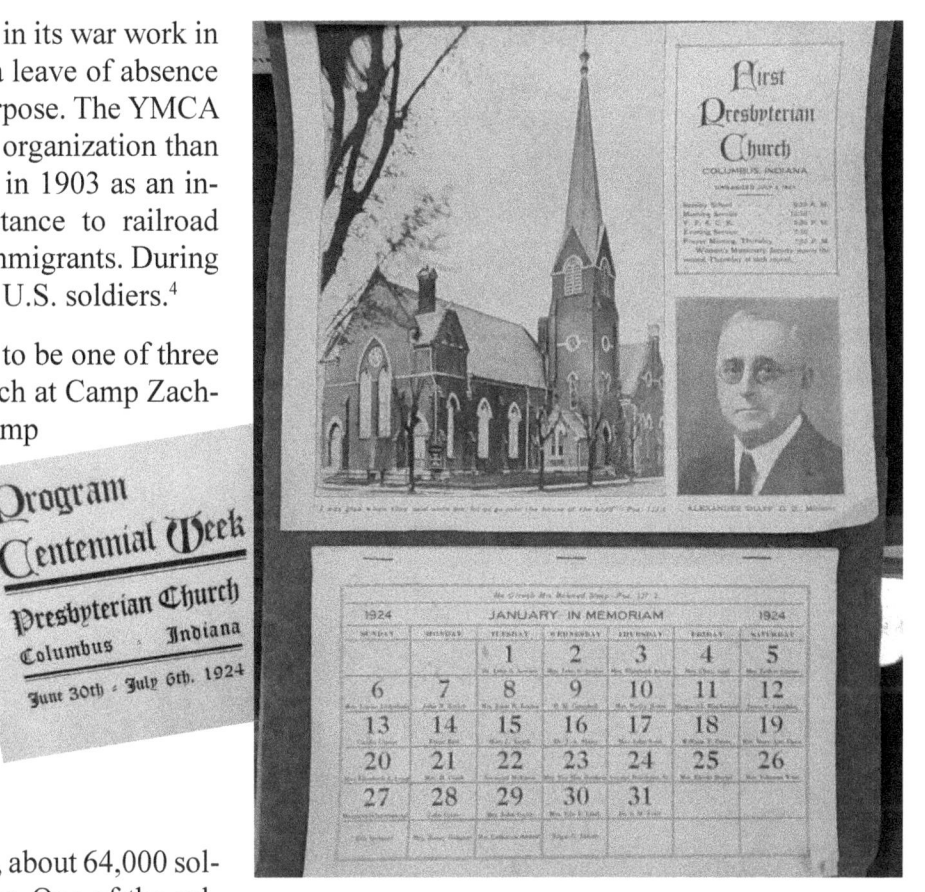

First Presbyterian celebrated its centennial while Alexander E. Sharp Sr. was its minister.

Sharp promoted cooperation among all denominations. When the Catholic priest died, he and the Rev. George H. Murphy, of the Methodist Church, attended the funeral together, at Sharp's suggestion. The Klan alleged it was Murphy's idea. Although Sharp set the record straight, the Klan forced Murphy's resignation. It had also caused the resignation of the Baptist minister and one or two others. The Indiana Klan's influence began to wane in the late 1920s.

\*\*\*

---
4 *YMCA*, https://www.ymca.org/who-we-are/our-history/1900s
5 *Louisville Courier-Journal*, Dec. 6, 2014.

# 200 YEARS of FIRST PRESBYTERIAN CHURCH of COLUMBUS, INDIANA

In 1924, the congregation had a week-long celebration of its centennial anniversary. The 100th anniversary events started on Monday, June 30, with representatives of the synod and presbytery speaking. On Tuesday, speakers included representatives of the Columbus Ministerial Association, as well as ministers from Edinburgh, Franklin, and Hopewell. Different organizations within the church gave presentations on Wednesday. Former ministers were presented and honored on the 100th birthday, Thursday, July 3. Friday saw an all-day picnic conducted at Donner Park, including a pageant. After a day of rest on Saturday, a special Communion service was held on Sunday.

The Centennial Committee published a booklet for the occasion. It included photos of previous ministers, elders, and those members who had entered the ministry; a historical sketch of the congregation; and a schedule of events.

*Alexander E. Sharp Sr. and his wife, Alethea, preparing to leave Columbus at the end of his tenure as pastor in 1932.*

\*\*\*

Three years later, the church dedicated the first addition to the original building, an L-shaped, two-story extension on the east and north sides of the Assembly (formerly Lecture) Room, consisting of a new minister's study, a kitchen and several classrooms.

Sharp received a Doctor of Divinity degree from Hanover College in 1920. He was elected moderator of the Synod of Indiana and served on its committee on education.[6] He was also president of the county ministerial association.[7] His wife taught German at Columbus High School.[8]

In 1932, he was called to be superintendent of the Estelle Peabody Memorial Home in North Manchester, one of the earliest of such Presbyterian-run retirement homes. A farewell service was organized by the local ministerial association and conducted at the Methodist church on the evening of Sept. 11 with other area congregations participating. The church was packed with well-wishers.

Sharp spoke at the gathering, saying, "I have participated gladly in many farewell meetings in this community, but never before have I realized what it meant to the one leaving." He spoke of his work here before crediting his wife for any accomplishment he may have made.[9]

Frank N. Richman, who was a member of the committee that called Sharp in 1910, later said that hiring him "was the best thing I ever did for this city."[10]

Sharp also held pastorates in Mingo Junction and Barberton, Ohio, and spent much of his retirement years at the Thornton Place for Presbyterian ministers in Newburgh, near Evansville, before it closed. His final two years were at Welborn Baptist Hospital in Evansville. He died Aug. 16, 1969.[11] [12]

---

6 *The Indianapolis News,* Feb. 23, 1927.
7 *The Evening Republican,* Sept. 6, 1927.
8 *The Evening Republican,* Sept. 7, 1918.
9 *The Evening Republican,* Sept. 12, 1932.
10 *The Evening Republican,* July 28, 1932.
11 *The Columbus Herald,* Aug. 22, 1969.
12 *Evansville Press,* June 27, 1967.

**FIRST PRESBYTERIAN CHURCH**
Columbus, Indiana
Dr. Alexander Sharp, Minister

## PLEDGE

Trusting in the Lord Jesus Christ for strength, I promise Him that I will strive to do whatever He would like to have me do; that I will make it the rule of my life to pray and read the Bible every day and to support my own church in every way, especially by attending all her regular Sunday and mid-week services, unless prevented by some reason which I can conscientiously give to my Savior and that just so far as I know how, throughout my whole life. I will endeavor to lead a Christian life. As an active member I promise to be true to all my duties, to be present at and to take some part aside from singing in every Christian Endeavor meeting, unless hindered by some reason which I can conscientiously give to my Lord and Master.

If obliged to be absent from the monthly consecration meeting of the society, I will, if possible, send at least a verse of scripture to be read in response to my name at roll call.

## BENEDICTION

The Lord watch between me and thee when are absent one from another.

---

Besides our Sunday evening (Christian Endeavor) meetings, we attended weekend retreats in Franklin, Greencastle and several in Indianapolis. It was always inspiring to get together with similar groups for discussions. Our group went to Heflin Camp at times for a day or two retreat. I also attended week-long retreats for young people at Hanover College two summers.

—Marian Dunlap

# Following in Father's Footsteps

**When Alexander Sharp's resignation** was offered at a congregational meeting in July 1932 following 22 years in the pulpit here, the congregation immediately called his son, Alexander E. Sharp, also known as Alexander Sharp Jr., as pastor. To have a son succeed a father in a pastorate is surely a rare happening anywhere and unique in our church history. The younger Sharp continued his father's liberal views of religion and community relations.

Tall and slender, Alexander E. Sharp Jr. was a student pastor at Christ Presbyterian Church in Madison, Wisconsin, at the time he was called to Columbus. He worked with students from the nearby University of Wisconsin.[1] He'd graduated from Columbus High School and Hanover College and studied for a year at the University of Edinburgh in Scotland.[2] He married Mary Elizabeth Sager not long before taking over the pastorate here.[3]

He spent seven years as pastor here, during which time the congregation was seen as "progressive, liberal and cooperative in community affairs." During these Depression years, the church was committed to efforts to help the impoverished.

Sharp was particularly concerned with the social needs of the young people during this stressful time. He was involved with Christian Endeavor, organized in 1881, under which TUXIS (U and I in Training and Service with Christ) was established, the emphasis being on fellowship as well as education. Dancing and pool were introduced, creating some outrage in the community of ministers.

Dancing caused Sharp's resignation as president of the local ministerial association. A New Year's party given by the TUXIS club of the Presbyterian church on Dec. 28, 1936, caused a kerfuffle because dancing was allowed at an event for youths. The party, held at the Columbus Chamber of Commerce, had gained the approval of the session (ruling board of the church). Sharp and two elders of the church served as chaperones. About 100 teens were present for the event, which included music by Emmert Wright's orchestra, confetti, serpentine, hats, balloons, horns, punch and cake ... and of all things, dancing![4]

When the local ministerial association caught wind of this development, some of the other members expressed embarrassment at having Sharp be their president. The association held a special meeting two days after the party, a meeting Sharp did not attend. He was invited to come before the association the following day but refused the invitation and sent a letter of resignation instead. When asked about the matter by a reporter, Sharp laughed and said:

"While world wars brew, while our own slums spread their germs through the city, while drunken driving stalks the highways, while strikes infest industry with millions of its workers unemployed, and while young people go off to college and laugh

*Alexander E. Sharp Jr.*

---

1 *The Capital Times*, Madison, Wis., Jan. 30, 1932.
2 *The Evening Republican*, July 28, 1932.
3 *The Evening Republican*, Oct. 29, 1989.
4 *The Evening Republican,* Dec. 29, 1936.

# 200 YEARS of FIRST PRESBYTERIAN CHURCH of COLUMBUS, INDIANA

> "It is amusing that some of our religious leaders have nothing more to do than attempt to 'church' the Presbyterian church for a holiday party given by one of its groups held entirely off church premises."
>
> — Alexander E. Sharp Jr.

up their sleeves at the church's refusal to face realities, it is amusing that some of our religious leaders have nothing more to do than attempt to 'church' the Presbyterian church for a holiday party given by one of its groups held entirely off church premises."[5]

An opinion piece a parent of a partygoer submitted to *The Evening Republican* addressed the situation, saying first that Sharp "is doing an unprecedented amount of good with the young people of the town, of all denominations. And I'm positive had all the parents in town seen this TUX-IS party, they, in a body, most likely would swamp Dr. Sharp, entreating him to continue his interest in their girls and boys."

The letter further said:

"If you belong to a church having a law saying 'no dancing,' you should not dance. An individual church law, however, does not make something sinful for someone who does not belong to that particular church."

The letter went on to state that with all the important issues going on in the world, this one did not deserve to be brought into the spotlight.

"The hullabaloo is merely a difference of opinion, not a 'moral issue.' So, let's forget it, spending our time to much better advantage in the contemplation of tolerance, charity and the constitution of these United States."[6]

Alexander E. Sharp Jr. and his wife, Mary, leaving Chicago en route to Columbus.

It is interesting to note that the elders of First Presbyterian dismissed Harriet Hayes for dancing in the early 1880s, showing how times change.

A few years after Sharp's so-called transgression, Presbyterians, especially the new pastor, Harold W. Turpin, and elder Gordon Ritter, were largely responsible for getting dancing approved for high school functions in Columbus. The first dance sanctioned by the local school administration was held on Nov. 26, 1943, at the armory following the Columbus vs. Franklin high school boys basketball game. The dance was for high school students only and ran from 9:30 p.m. to 12:30 a.m. Several student dances had been conducted recently, but they were not under the sponsorship of the school administration or any other organization.[7]

---

5  *The Evening Republican,* Jan. 4, 1937.
6  *The Evening Republican,* Jan. 5, 1937.
7  *The Evening Republican,* Nov. 26, 1943.

# 200 YEARS of FIRST PRESBYTERIAN CHURCH of COLUMBUS, INDIANA

Other innovations under Sharp were a Little Theater group, a Sunday school orchestra and a men's work group. He wanted everyone to feel comfortable in church, so smoking was allowed in the men's Sunday school class. (In acknowledgment of the health hazards of smoking, the church went smoke free again many years ago.)

In 1936, like his father before him, Sharp Jr. was awarded an honorary Doctor of Divinity degree by Hanover College. The Synod of Indiana asked him to take the duties of Indiana secretary of the church's national mission, and he resigned his Columbus pastorate to take that position in August 1939.

After serving the synod for 10 years, he was administrative secretary for the Board of National Missions of the Presbyterian Church for 14 years. He retired in 1970 and died in 1989 in Atlanta at 86 years of age.[8]

\*\*\*

The first Sunday after Sharp left, there were no services at the church. A pulpit committee headed by A. W. Phillips was two months into its search for Sharp's replacement but hadn't come to a decision yet.[9] It wasn't long before Sharp's father, who had retired not long before, agreed to return and fill in on an interim basis. He did just that until the congregation called Harold W. Turpin, who came from a pastorate at Indianapolis Seventh Presbyterian Church, to begin work as pastor on Jan. 7, 1940.[10]

Turpin continued the liberal theology and community involvement of his predecessors. Although it was a controversial act at the time, he organized the first chapter of Alcoholics Anonymous in Columbus, and the group met in the church for more than three decades.

Turpin attended a six-week school of alcohol studies at Yale University in the summer of 1943 as a representative of the Indiana Council of Churches. In September of that year, he preached a sermon on the organization during services one Sunday.[11] By February 1944, a local chapter had been set up and was running advertisements in the papers, soliciting those with alcohol issues to seek help. Turpin spoke on AA at other churches and at meetings of clubs and organizations.

Harold W. Turpin

> "He (Harold Turpin) called at our house many times. In fact, we dubbed him 'the callingest on members' minster we had encountered."
>
> – Warren Phillips

One hundred years earlier, Presbyterians were in the forefront of a women's prayer vigil in front of the town's most notorious saloon. If this was an effort to get the saloon closed, it singularly failed, but it did lead to the establishment of a local chapter of the Woman's Christian Temperance Union, which was still flourishing in the 1940s.

Although the Ku Klux Klan had long ceased to be a factor in Columbus, the city was still almost completely segregated. When the adult Bible class decided to study problems concerning race relationships, Turpin invited Grant Smith, a barber who owned the Palace Barber and Beauty Shop and the Basement Barber Shop and an able Bible student, to teach one of the lessons. Smith, a Black man, was astonished at the invitation, for he had never been invited to a "white" church, but he accepted and was well-received.

Calling on members was a specialty of Turpin. "He called at our house many times," wrote member Warren Phillips in 2001. "In fact, we dubbed him 'the callingest on members' minster we had encountered."

Turpin was elected chairman of the pastors' section of the quadrennial convention of Christian education, held Feb. 9 to

---

8   *The Evening Republican,* Oct. 29, 1989.
9   *The Evening Republican,* Sept. 2, 1939.
10  *The Evening Republican*, Jan. 5, 1940.
11  *The Evening Republican*, Sept. 10, 1943.

# 200 YEARS of FIRST PRESBYTERIAN CHURCH of COLUMBUS, INDIANA

The First Presbyterian Church choir program has been magnificent for years. At one time, the church had four choirs, ranging from adult to primary school. In 1946, Theodore (Ted) Hunt was hired as our first minister of music.

11, 1942, in Chicago. This section was the second largest of the 16 at the convention, which was attended by 1,800 people from all over the United States and Canada. He presented a program on education through fellowship and recreation and based it on the subject "The Church and the USO (United Service Organizations)."[12]

Turpin's last sermon at First Presbyterian was spoken on July 10, 1949, the last day of the church's 125th anniversary week celebration and the 18th anniversary of his ordination. His next job was pastor at First United Presbyterian Church in Hammond, where he stayed for 17 years. Turpin, who had attended Rankin Presbyterian Church in Brush, Colorado, as a child, pastored that same church from 1966 to 1979. He died at his home in Paducah, Kentucky, in 1993 at the age of 88.[13]

\*\*\*

From sometime in the late 19th century until the mid-1970s, when staff members elected to divide their vacation time throughout the year, it was the custom at many Presbyterian churches across the country for the minister to take the month of August for vacation, the "August vacation" as it was termed. Columbus was no exception.

In the 1920s, when the First Methodist minister was away in July, the two congregations worshipped together during the summer. In the 1930s, there were no morning services, but the congregation took part in a community outdoor vesper service each Sunday evening. In 1944, at the behest of the Board of Deacons, Sunday morning services resumed in August, with supply preachers, but in 1948 an elder proposed that "church services be suspended in the month of August as a vacation for the entire congregation." The motion carried, and there were no church activities in August for the next two years.

\*\*\*

World War II brought the church an influx of families from all over the country who were stationed at Camp Atterbury and Atterbury Army Air Force Base (later renamed Bakalar Air Force Base). Camp Atterbury, an Army camp carved out of 40,000 acres of land 12 miles north of Columbus, was built in response to Japan's attack on Pearl Harbor, Dec. 7, 1941. Six months after

---

12  *The Evening Republican*, Feb. 12, 1942.
13  *The Paducah (Ky.) Sun*, Sept. 14, 1993.

# 200 YEARS of FIRST PRESBYTERIAN CHURCH of COLUMBUS, INDIANA

Left: The Donner House was completed in 1949. Below: Children play volleyball in the gym.

construction started in February 1942, soldiers started arriving. At its peak, the camp hosted more than 44,000 officers and soldiers.[14] The Air Force base, meanwhile, was built 4 miles north of Columbus at the site of present-day Columbus Municipal Airport between August and December 1942.

The increase in military families stayed even into the 1950s. At one point, the Laws family took in an Army couple for several weeks until they could find a home.

\*\*\*

In the years immediately after the war, the congregation took two major strides. In 1946, Theodore (Ted) Hunt was named as the first minister of music, serving part time until 1961. He established a five-choir program: primary, junior, junior high, senior high and adult. In Turpin's words, "the ministry of music program was revived and thrived after we brought Ted Hunt into the picture."

Hunt held several other musical positions in Columbus over a span of nearly 50 years. He played viola in the Columbus Symphony Orchestra for 41 years, was organist and choirmaster at St. Paul's Episcopal Church for 19 years and organist at Hathaway-Myers Funeral Home for 11 years, to name a few.[15]

\*\*\*

Eventually, it was purported that something should be done about the need for more classrooms and a multipurpose fellowship room, ideas that had been shelved during the war years.

The path to getting money to pay for such additions started several years earlier. In 1935, after the death of his mother, William H. Donner, son of Frederick and Mary Donner, gave the family home (directly across Franklin Street) to the church in memory of his parents, who had been longtime members. The house was sold in 1940 to Indiana Bell Telephone Co., which razed it and built a facility to help usher in dial telephones in the city.[16] Part of the proceeds from the home sale went to buy land just north of the church.

A building fund was later established, and Jerald Dunlap, owner of a construction company and member of the congregation, was asked to develop a design. When William Donner, then residing in Philadelphia, heard of the plans, he contributed $95,000 to the effort as a memorial to his parents; the congregation raised the remaining $30,000.[17] Completed in 1949 and dedicated in March 1950, the Donner Church House was a red-brick, two-story building approximately 77-by-120 feet. It contained six large rooms on the lower floor: a youth room, Sunday school rooms, women's reception parlor and a kitchenette. A gymnasium/auditorium, with a fully equipped stage and

---

14  Riker, Dorothy, ed. *The Hoosier Training Ground: A History of Army and Navy Training Centers, Forts, Depots, and Other Military Installations Within the State Boundaries During World War II. Indiana in World War II. Vol. III.* Bloomington: Indiana War History Commission. Pp. 23-24. 1952.
15  *The Republic*, Oct. 12, 1995.
16  *The Evening Republican*, July 20, 1940.
17  *The Evening Republican*, March 6, 1950.

projection room, was on the upper level. The auditorium seated up to 400 people.[18]

In the 1980s, Donner's youngest daughter, Dora Donner Ide, gave $40,000 toward replacing the heating system and completely renovating the lower floor of the Donner Building.

As the church entered the decade of the 1950s, retired minister Jesse Tidball was serving as interim pastor. He arrived from Madison, where he had served as minister for 24 years, in September 1949 to a newly painted church, one in which the drab gray of the entrance hall had been updated with golden-colored iron stair rails, a hue that looked similar to a natural wood finish.[19]

Soon the church would make its biggest hire to the pulpit yet.

---

18  *The Evening Republican,* March 4, 1950.
19  *The Evening Republican,* Aug. 30, 1949.

## Women Who Made a Difference

By Carrie Ong / 1954

Reprinted from Carol Berkey's 175th anniversary book

My name is Carrie Ong. I used to teach a few blocks down Seventh Street at Columbus High School. After 39 years in the classroom, I retired three years ago in 1951. Since then I have acted as church visitor, a marvelous opportunity to get to know new Presbyterians in town.

This year I have been given a singular honor by this congregation. I have been elected by you to the office of elder. For 140 years this office was reserved for men.

I consider this an honor not for myself alone but for all the women who have made a real difference in this congregation throughout its history.

When the church was organized in 1824, 13 of the 20 early members were women. In the 1840s, when the elders of the church believed the congregation was too small and too poor to build a church, the women raised the money.

Carrie Ong

The same thing happened when this building was put on hold because of monetary problems. The women came up with a great many fundraising events. And still today the Women's Association is actively raising money for church projects and missions. Countless meals have been prepared, served and cleaned up in our church kitchen.

The first woman who contributed much time and devotion to this church, of whom I personally was aware, was my mother, Anna Ong. She was for many years the organist – unpaid, of course. Later, Ida Edenburn gave countless hours as choir director.

— Continues on next page

# 200 YEARS of FIRST PRESBYTERIAN CHURCH of COLUMBUS, INDIANA

In the 1890s women of this church, Mary Donner, Elmira Brown, Grace Compton and Clara Hendricks, ventured into an area of town that might well have intimidated many men to bring the story of Jesus to the children living there. There was Miranda Hinman, who taught the nursery class (which at that time had all children to the age of 6) for 18 consecutive years, and Vida Newsom, who taught her girls' classes to be concerned with conserving the land God gave us. Ruth Shull was Sunday school secretary, and Jessie Cummins taught high school girls, both serving many years.

In 1946 when we hired Ted Hunt as minister of music, we may not have realized it was a two-for-one deal, but Sarah Hunt has made our Christian education program come alive since she took the chairmanship.

When church histories are written, they deal mostly with buildings and ministers. Little is said about the ministers' wives. But from Margaret Dickey to Ellen Laws, these women have contributed much. Margaret Dickey probably never set foot in Columbus. She lived on the frontier where Indians still roamed the woods, and she raised 11 children. She fully supported her husband's missionary work, which took him away from home for months at a time. He might not otherwise have established this church. Ellen Laws, in the nearly five years she has been here, has endeared herself to us and made countless contributions to the Women's Association and the church as a whole.

These are but a few of the women who have made a difference to this congregation. Many more teachers, choir members, committee members, workers on projects, from decorating the sanctuary for Christmas, to collecting and boxing blankets for missions to preparing the Communion elements, have served more or less anonymously but diligently and extremely well.

I am certain that I am only the _first_ woman elder and that there will soon be women deacons, too, maybe even trustees. And someday, who knows? – we even may have a woman as minister!

---

Carrie Ong, who became a member of First Presbyterian on Easter Sunday 1897, was indeed the first female elder at First Presbyterian Church. But she also made quite an impact outside the church walls. A lifelong resident of Columbus, she served as the city librarian, taught English at Columbus High School from 1912 to 1951, serving as head of the English department all but her first year. She served on many boards for local organizations and was the first female member of Columbus City Council, serving from 1956 to 1959. She died at the age of 74 on April 15, 1960, just five days after the Columbus Community School Board honored her by naming the old junior high school at Seventh and Pearl streets Carrie Ong Junior High School.

---

"We believe that God has called us to help and to do good for others. As we believe in Jesus, we've got to do that, and we've got to take that very seriously."

— Merry Carmichael, member since 1967,
from a 1996 story in The Republic

# 200 YEARS of FIRST PRESBYTERIAN CHURCH of COLUMBUS, INDIANA

The sanctuary in 1952 (top), 1969 (left), 1996 (right).

53

# Bill Laws: A Giant of a Man

**The first name** longtime congregation members – and many community members – mention when discussing pastors with a passion for social justice is still Bill Laws.

Both a leader in religious and civic circles, William Robert Laws Jr. was elected moderator of the General Assembly of Presbyterian Churches USA, the highest office in the Presbyterian Church, in 1970. For his civic contributions he earned the Community Service Award in 1975 from the Columbus Area Chamber of Commerce. He initiated or was associated with numerous activities designed to meet the needs of people.

> "Bill Laws was one of the finest human beings who has ever lived in Columbus."
>
> — J. Irwin Miller

"Bill Laws was one of the finest human beings who has ever lived in Columbus," said J. Irwin Miller, former chairman of Cummins Engine Co., upon Laws' death in 1985.

In the nearly 50 years since he left the pulpit after a 26-year stint as minister at First Presbyterian, Laws' footsteps were deemed quite large by those who succeeded him.

"When he left, I felt the burden and the potential of the opportunity for me to continue as pastor," recalled Warner M. Bailey, who replaced Laws as pastor in 1976. "I will always remember a well-meaning member coming into my office on the first day of my new role and telling me that pastors who take over from someone who has had a long and beloved tenure frequently are fired and leave the ministry. What a way to begin!"

The Rev. William R. (Bill) Laws spent 26 years in the First Presbyterian pulpit, either as pastor or co-pastor. His contributions to the church and the community still resonate today, nearly 50 years after he retired.

## 200 YEARS of FIRST PRESBYTERIAN CHURCH of COLUMBUS, INDIANA

A North Carolina native, Bill Laws came to First Presbyterian in 1950 from Buechel Presbyterian Church in what was then a suburb of Louisville, Kentucky. At right: Laws with children at the baptismal font.

Today's pastor, Felipe Martinez, came to understand Laws' significance early on in his time here.

"When I first heard of Bill Laws, I thought, 'Boy, how do I live under that guy's shadow?'" Martinez said.

Fortunately for Martinez, he found out the job wasn't to be placed entirely on the pastor's shoulders.

"I realized that it's how do *we* live up to his legacy? Or how do *we* share the vision?" Martinez said.

\*\*\*

Laws' legacy and vision were as big as his persona. He was 6 feet, 4 inches tall with a deep voice, wasn't afraid to look people in the eye, asked direct questions and gave direct answers, while all the time giving the impression of genuineness.

David M. Liddle Jr., who served as a minister here for almost two decades, from 1982 to 1997, said of Laws, "I learned early on that during his ministry he'd attained legendary status as a preacher, pastor and community leader. He had a booming voice that got your attention, but also the ability to connect with people on a personal level, whether friends or strangers."

"He was a kind, thoughtful, deep-thinking individual; he was nonjudgmental," said Pat Bush, who along with her husband, Ben, had been Methodists until being invited to hear Laws preach at First Presbyterian.

"Bill Laws was a super minister to grow up with, in my opinion," Skip Lindemann said. "He seemed 'real' to me and did not put on false smiles and other stuff."

Not that Laws' directness might not have made some a tad ill at ease now and then.

55

# 200 YEARS of FIRST PRESBYTERIAN CHURCH of COLUMBUS, INDIANA

"He was scary; Laws scared me to death," Vern Jorck said with a laugh. "We discussed big topics at the presbytery. Afterward, he would stare into your eyes and look right through you and ask you, 'What do you think?' There was no question more fearful for me than asking me what I think.'"

Liddle agreed that Laws could be quite direct in his approach. "If he met you on the street, for example, instead of the conventional greeting, 'How are you?' he might greet you with a probing question like, 'How are you *deep down*?' ... and expect an answer!"

"I asked him what predestination meant," said member Larry Long. "His answer was great with his modest understatement, 'I can't really explain it, and it really doesn't matter. So don't worry about it.'"

Liddle added that Laws "was beloved by many and had even earned the respect, albeit sometimes grudging, of those who thought him to be too progressive or too political."

> "(He) was beloved by many and had even earned the respect, albeit sometimes grudging, of those who thought him to be too progressive or too political."
> — David Liddle Jr.

Of her husband, Ellen wrote some years after he passed away: "Bill considered his work 'evangelistic' – telling the good news, and his task to bring the congregation along to do their part in spreading the good news where they were situated. This was a day-to-day and never-ending effort. It underlay all programs and efforts and had little to do with the big tent meetings most people connect with the word 'evangelism.'"

Laws' leadership skills were well developed before coming to Columbus in 1950.

\*\*\*

> "Bill considered his work 'evangelistic' – telling the good news, and his task to bring the congregation along to do their part in spreading the good news where they were situated. ... It had little to do with the big tent meetings most people connect with the word 'evangelism.'"
> — Ellen Laws

Born Aug. 18, 1916, in Durham, North Carolina, he was a graduate of Davidson College in Davidson, North Carolina, before attending Louisville Presbyterian Seminary.

"My dad (A.D. Ellison) was in seminary with Bill in Louisville in the early 1940s," Zack Ellison said. "Even then, he was considered a leader in the seminary."

In Louisville Laws married Ellen a few weeks before graduation in 1943. It was also in that area that a search committee from Columbus heard Laws preach at Buechel Presbyterian Church, impressing the committee to such a degree that it was convinced to offer him the opportunity to move north and lead First Presbyterian here.

"After hearing numerous sermons in Presbyterian churches for the last six months," a story in the Jan. 10, 1950, Evening Republican stated, "the committee of the local church looking for a minister to its flock finally was bowled over by the engaging qualities of

## 200 YEARS of FIRST PRESBYTERIAN CHURCH of COLUMBUS, INDIANA

the Rev. William R. Laws of a suburban congregation of Louisville."

A member of that search committee, Waldo Harrison, wrote in this church's book celebrating 175 years about going to Buechel (since annexed into Louisville) to see Laws. "We had heard good things about him, so we went to … hear him preach. The committee split up, taking seats in different parts of the sanctuary so that we wouldn't be too obvious. Bill says we stuck out like sore thumbs."

Members of the committee were impressed.

"What a preacher!" Harrison wrote.

Bill Laws

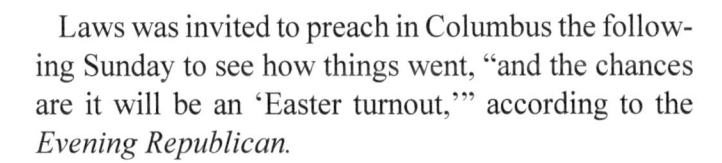

\*\*\*

Laws was invited to preach in Columbus the following Sunday to see how things went, "and the chances are it will be an 'Easter turnout,'" according to the *Evening Republican*.

He was installed as pastor in Columbus during special services held on March 1, 1950, a Wednesday evening. The following Sunday, his first with his new title, coincided with a formal presentation and dedication of the Donner House, the new church annex and recreation building. His sermon, titled "The Challenge of this Hour," was based upon the future use of the building.

"I consider one of the most important things I have ever done was serving on the committee that called Bill Laws to be minister of this church," Harrison said.

The congregation thought it was going to lose Laws immediately after his wife and daughters, Marty and Anne, arrived on Feb. 28. A near blizzard the next day sent shivers through the normally well-maintained manse at 1039 Franklin St. that the church's pastors lived in.

"We were pretty proud of our manse," Harrison wrote, noting that it had been built in 1902 and remodeled in 1936. The house had been empty since summer, but "the trustees did all the necessary things — cleaning and painting, etc. — to get it ready for the new family. Well, that manse nearly lost us our new pastor four days after he arrived! You have to remember that those were the days before Thermopane windows, or

---

"The committee of the local church looking for a minister to its flock finally was bowled over by the engaging qualities of the Rev. William R. Laws of a suburban congregation of Louisville."

— The Evening Republican // Jan. 10, 1950

anyone gave much thought to insulation. Somehow or other, the storm windows and doors had not been put up that year — how did we overlook that?"

As Laws later said, "You could see the rugs dance on the floor," Harrison said.

After the storm, both the girls got sick. A day later, the family was ready to head back to Kentucky.

To make matters worse, Harrison said, the nation was in the middle of a coal miners' strike, and there was no coal to be bought in Columbus. There was only about half a bin of coal for the furnace at the manse, and Laws was worried that it would be depleted in the extremely cold weather. Claude Combs, a trustee and owner of a coal company, assured him that, if necessary, coal would be moved to the manse from the bin at the church.

"So we weathered that crisis, and the Laws family stayed," Harrison wrote.

\*\*\*

It didn't take long before Laws became entrenched in the First Presbyterian and Columbus communities. He quickly became a highly visible and vocal advocate for such causes as open housing, racial equality and integration of public facilities, as well as educational opportunities for all.

The congregation was so enamored of its leader that for Christmas 1951, it presented Laws a month's trip to Palestine, which he took in April of the following year with the American Christian Palestine committee. He also spent some time in Paris, Rome, Egypt, Jordan and Israel and upon his return, presented travelogues of his journey to city, church and civic organizations.

More praise heaped on Laws for his early efforts in leading this congregation came in a Nov. 18, 1954, story in the *Evening Republican*: "It wasn't long after Rev. Laws assumed his duties … until the congregation was re-awakened, so to speak. The Presbyterians, who had been 'church goers' for many years, were more than ever intent on attending church because they were afraid if they didn't, they might miss something, namely Rev. Laws' sermons."

Laws had a way of injecting witticisms to take the sharp edge off his messages, while still making the seriousness stick.

"I liked him," said Cal Brand, who moved to Columbus with his family as a 7-year-old the year before Laws arrived. "I remember one (of his sermons) clearly. He was talking about God's love, and he used an image from boxing. He said no matter how often you get a shot in, God absorbs it and doesn't hit back. I'm not sure he said it exactly that way, but that's how I remember it."

Laws would also preach that we must take responsibility for our own actions, Brand said. "He said, 'If you can cut all the trees down on the riverbank, and if it floods the next year, it's your own fault.'"

\*\*\*

Laws brought in folks from outside the congregation for discussions. Early in his tenure here he started a "Koffee Klass" for adults following service, where he'd enlighten people with varied backgrounds on their obligations in the community, the mechanism of the church government, the duties of local church officers and more.

While the congregation and its individual members had always been active in community affairs, Laws' arrival led to even more leadership roles for congregants wherever they saw a need.

In a November 1954 interview with the *Evening Republican*, Laws stated that Columbus had "an un-

> "It wasn't long after Rev. Laws assumed his duties ... until the congregation was re-awakened, so to speak."
>
> — The Evening Republican

derstandable pride, an obvious outward success in many areas, with the result that individuals and some groups of people have been ignored, hurt."

\*\*\*

In 1956, like his predecessors Alexander Sharp and Alexander E. Sharp, Laws was awarded an honorary Doctor of Divinity degree by Hanover College. First Presbyterian's ties to Hanover have been close since John M. Dickey was named first president of the college board of trustees in 1833.

\*\*\*

Ben Bush took many trips around the presbytery with Laws. On those drives, Laws often discussed his affinity for the Rev. Martin Luther King Jr., an American Baptist minister, activist and political philosopher who was one of the most prominent leaders in the civil rights movement from 1955 until his assassination in 1968.

This was an indication of Laws' interest in racial equality, an issue he saw firsthand growing up in North Carolina. His actions matched his words. He was one of the leading forces in getting local barbershops to integrate. He and some other community leaders were also instrumental in integrating apartment complexes in Columbus.

The Rev. Martin Luther King Jr. and the fight for Blacks to achieve civil rights held special places in Bill Laws' heart. // Pixabay

George Newlin said in a 1985 interview with *The Republic* that when it came to improving race relations in Columbus, Laws was "effective because most of us recognized that coming from North Carolina, he was going through some of the same things we were going through."

Not all the congregation went along with these plans for racial equality. While the Ku Klux Klan was for all intents and purposes gone from Columbus, much racial prejudice remained, including among some Presbyterians. When Ted Hunt wanted to invite Versie Booker, a Black woman, to sing in the choir in 1958, Laws' only question was, "Can she sing?" She indeed could, having built a local reputation. But there was some opposition, a minority but quite vocal, and Booker sang here only briefly. Fifteen years later, First Presbyterian had several African American families, all active in the church, with an elder, a couple of deacons and two choir members.

> "He (Laws) opened our church to those who might otherwise not want to come there."
>
> – George Newlin

"He opened our church to those who might otherwise not want to come there," Newlin said.

When these families left the congregation, usually by moving from Columbus, the church attracted few other Black families.

One of Cal Brand Jr.'s favorite youth group activities involved Laws getting the children together with some other youth groups and taking them to Indianapolis to see "Porgy and Bess," a play about African Americans living in poverty in Charleston, South Carolina, in the 1920s.

"That was a mind blower; it was a real eye opener," Brand said.

Ellen Laws thought it interesting that when the couple came to Columbus, "Bill used to chuckle ruefully that … First Presbyterian was seen by some as *the* church to belong to." Later, after dealing with racial issues ... and other tense moments, it became "Oh, *that* church," she wrote. "For some, that was painful treatment, for others a recognition that the church was active where it should be and trying to deal with problems in the community in a responsible manner. Some people have been drawn to the church *because* of the work it does and the stands it takes in the community."

\*\*\*

During Laws' time here the congregation established the Presbyterian Foundation for the purpose of receiving bequests, memorials and other gifts and expending such funds to promote religious, educational and charitable purposes.

The church also:

• Opened the first preschool in town; it still exists.

• Opened a child care center that eventually became Children Inc.

• Started a program to allow young mothers and mothers-to-be to finish their educations.

• Grew to the point that a second Presbyterian church in Columbus – Fairlawn Presbyterian – opened.

• Hired its first full-time minister of music.

• Assumed leadership of Love Chapel, a small church in a less affluent section of East Columbus and started a FISH program, providing food for needy families.

• Started a Child Care Clinic and the Emergency Assistance Fund.

• Shared its sanctuary with St. Bartholomew Catholic Church in 1975, when that church was undergoing a complete remodeling.

• Accepted sponsorship of families of refugees from Cuba, Laos and Vietnam.

In 1969, to commemorate his 20th year as minister, Laws was given sabbatical leave. He and Ellen went to San Francisco, where he enrolled at the San Francisco Presbyterian Seminary for the fall semester.

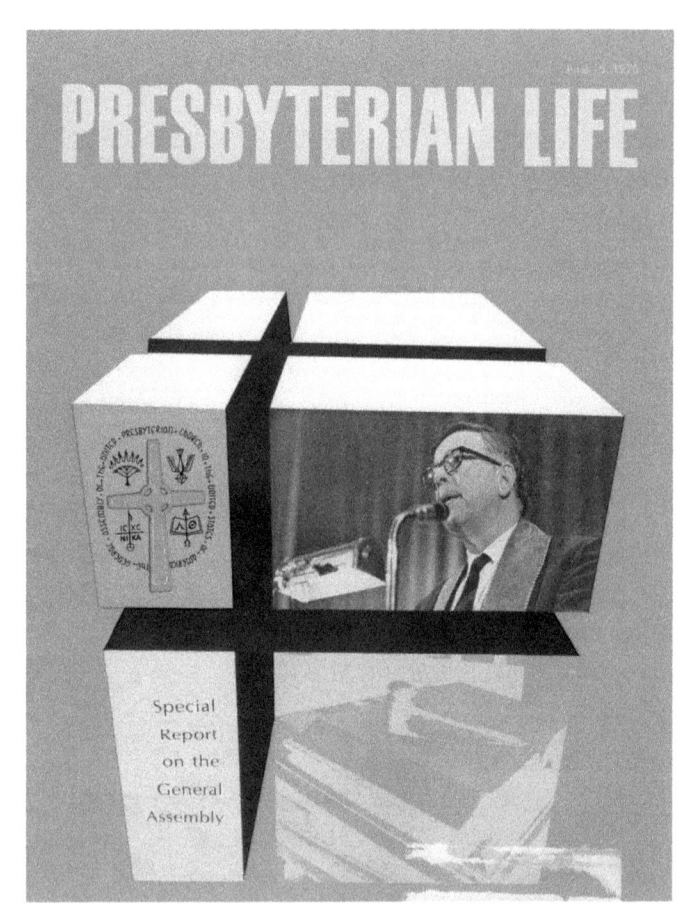

\*\*\*

Bill Laws graced the cover of "Presbyterian Life" magazine after being elected moderator of the 182nd General Assembly in 1970.

While Laws had made a name for himself and his church for several years, it wasn't until May 20, 1970, when the entire United Presbyterian Church in the United States of America took notice. That's when he was elected moderator of the 182nd General Assembly. The moderator was responsible for presiding over the meeting of the General Assembly, a weeklong event held annually, and serving as an ambassador of the denomination throughout the remainder of the year-long term.

Heading to the General Assembly meeting that year, Laws had been endorsed by the Presbytery of Indianapolis and the General Council of the Synod of Indiana as a candidate for moderator. He was also selected as a commissioner for the General Assembly, along with fellow First Presbyterian member Ben Bush. About 800 commissioners were charged with electing the moderator to lead its 3.2-million-member church for a year. Four other men had their hats in the moderator ring: James Bell, London, Ohio; the Rev. Charles R. Everhardt, Phoenix; the Rev. Elmer George Homrighausen, Princeton, N.J.; and the Rev. A.L. Reynolds, Chicago.

The Columbus committee nominating Laws, headed by Waldo Harrison and also featuring Ben and Pat Bush in prominent roles, provided promotional materials to the commissioners in support of their candidate. The assembly also allowed a two-minute nominating speech and a one-minute seconding speech for each candidate.

Among the reasons the local nominating committee told commissioners Laws would make a great moderator were:

This page and next page: Promotional materials touting Bill Laws as a candidate for moderator at the 182nd General Assembly of the United Presbyterian Church in the United States of America in Chicago. Laws won on the second ballot.

### The Man with Leadership for This Assembly

#### THE MAN

He inspires unity and brotherhood in a congregation consisting of persons from multiracial and ethnic origins . . . From his pulpit he proclaims the message that we are to live before God as if He were the only one who matters, and that all we are is a consequence of His selection, His judgment, and His graciousness.

Born in Durham, N. Carolina, August 18, 1916; Educated at Davidson College, Davidson, N. C. Graduated cum laude (B.A.) 1938; and Louisville Seminary, Louisville, Ky. (B.D.) 1943; Hanover College (Honorary D.D.) 1956; Louisville Seminary Scholars Program 1963; Sabbatical study San Francisco Seminary, San Anselmo, California studying crisis periods in church history, Christian Ethics and Communicating the Christian Faith. 1969-70.

He and his wife Ellen have two daughters, Margaret and Anne. His ministry has been to the congregations of the Beuchel Presbyterian Church, Louisville, Ky., and First United Presbyterian Church, Columbus, Indiana.

#### HIS LEADERSHIP

A pre-school center was opened to all families in the community.
A literacy program for teaching adults to read and write was established as a community-wide project.
Organized and now assists in a ministry to migrant workers living in the community.
Sponsored a Cuban refugee family.
Established the first Community Day Care Center in Columbus, Ind.
Provided facilities for Alcoholics Anonymous and assists in supporting this program with counseling.
Instrumental in establishing a foundation for under-privileged students of all races in need of personal help and encouragement to continue higher education.
Helped to sponsor a series of five Ecumenical Dialogues in the community.
Provided the colonizing body for a second church, and also supported the second church financially during the early years. The co-operation of the two congregations is firmly established.

#### HIS APPROACH

"Reconciliation is not the same as unanimity of opinion. Cornelius did not cease to be a Roman nor a military man. Peter did not cease being a Jew nor a citizen of an occupied country. Yet they were one in Jesus Christ."

To this concept of unity, Bill is deeply committed, seeking always to open opportunities for reconciliation to those holding divergent views. At a time when apprehension and anxiety are apparent, more than most, this man has the wisdom and capacity to serve as moderator with dignity and competence.

"To put it Biblically, I believe the church is God's people in the world; that is, a people whose style of life tells the world about the world's creator and lover and sovereign, and also a people who brings the world to God in loving and sacrificial concern. I believe the Church is therefore the bearer of the word of God in and to contemporary society."

# 200 YEARS of FIRST PRESBYTERIAN CHURCH of COLUMBUS, INDIANA

- He had great insight and breadth of knowledge.

- He could get to the heart of an issue and clarify divergent opinions so that people might "hear" one another.

- He had outstanding leadership skills.

It took two ballots for a candidate to receive more than the 50 percent threshold needed to win; on that ballot, Laws got 503 of the 805 votes, easily surpassing the 403 needed to be elected.

"Tell my friends in Columbus that I'm surprised to be here. I thought I was the dark-horse candidate," Laws said via telephone to a reporter from *The Republic* after his election. "Waldo and his committee got the job done.

"It is an exciting job," he added, "and one with a great deal of responsibility. While in office I want to emphasize the importance of the parish church and would like to see our denomination be faithful and responsible in these times of stress."

In his acceptance speech, Laws employed a bit of the wit he would often use while discussing serious subjects. He told the General Assembly, "Last Sunday my sermon to my congregation was entitled 'Reflections of a Moderatorial Candidate,' and I said to those Presbyterians, 'Don't pray for me; pray for the church.' My first sermon upon returning to Columbus will probably be entitled 'Reflections of a Recently Elected Moderator,' and I'm going to say, 'Keep on praying for the church, but begin to pray for me.'"

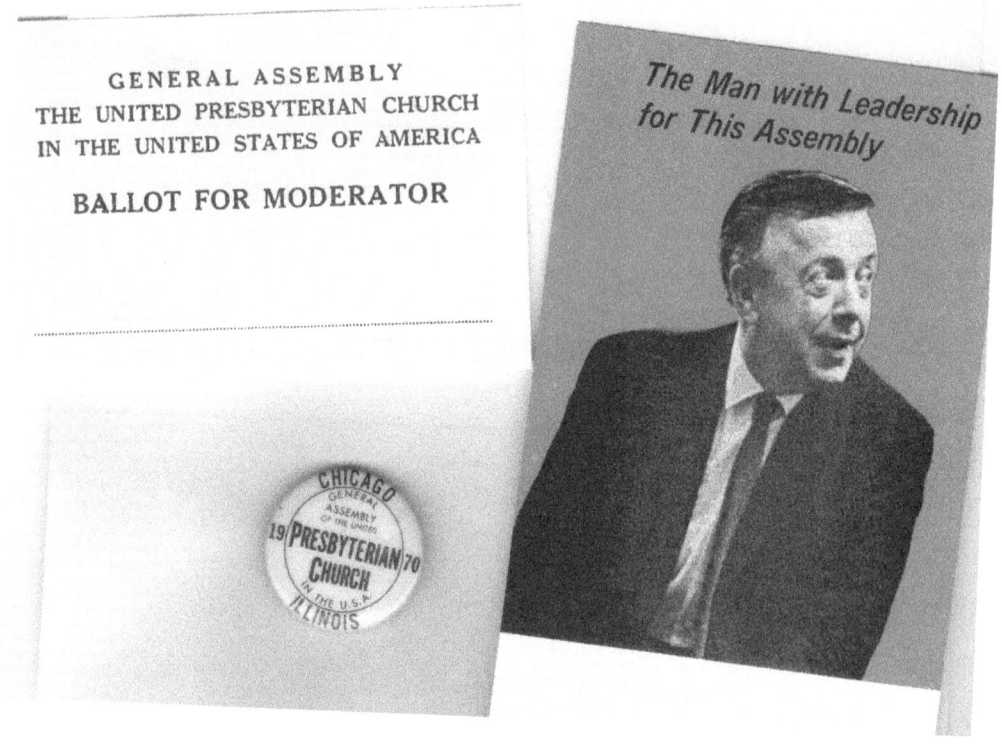

---

"I thought I was the dark-horse candidate. Waldo (Harrison) and his committee got the job done.

— The Rev. Bill Laws

# 200 YEARS of FIRST PRESBYTERIAN CHURCH of COLUMBUS, INDIANA

> "I think the church ought to be aware of where people are hurting and be prepared to stand in there and do something about it. The church has been compelled to become an interpreter and participant in social change. The church should be the bearer and expressor of what it means to be human ... to be a child of creation."
>
> — Rev. Bill Laws

Candidates had been questioned by the delegates prior to the vote. In answer to some of the questions, *The Republic* on June 12, 1970, quoted Laws as saying that he:

- Would not be in favor of sending young men into wars that had not been declared by the U.S. Congress.

- Would like to see the assembly "be so sophisticated and open in its integrity that it learns how to influence political decisions, because that's where the power is that's being exerted that's affecting human lives in our day."

- Saw the church as an agent of social change. "I think the church ought to be aware of where people are hurting and be prepared to stand in there and do something about it. The church has been compelled to become an interpreter and participant in social change. The church should be the bearer and expressor of what it means to be human ... to be a child of creation."

\*\*\*

The turbulent times of the late 1960s and early 1970s threatened to disrupt the assembly, but Laws managed to ease that threat, too. A group of young people calling themselves the Submarine Church, upset and angry with their country, planned to disrupt proceedings in Chicago as they had at the Methodist gathering in St. Louis a month prior. Laws was familiar with the group, consisting in part of students who had entered the seminary to avoid the draft and were against American involvement in the Vietnam War. Laws and his wife, Ellen, had met some of them during his sabbatical in 1969 in San Francisco.

Bill Laws, in ceremonial stole, following his investiture as moderator of the 182nd General Assembly in 1970.

In Chicago, a mutual acquaintance was able to get Laws and members of the group together for a chat in Grant Park along Lake Michigan, and he arranged for the group to have 30 minutes to present their arguments to the whole assembly. The fact that the very highest of authority figures would sit down with them and actually listen to their grievances was something they had not expected.

"To realize the church had listened, that at least some had even cared in spite of different opinions diffused their anger, ended their plans to be disruptive," Ellen Laws wrote years later.

The next day, the Submarine Church went to Second Presbyterian Church to hear Laws preach, had lunch with the Laws contingent at a nearby restaurant, and shared an informal communion, Ellen said.

"Looking back, it seemed to us that God's hand had been directing our path through the preceding months to prepare for those days," Ellen said.

This was a time the Vietnam War was getting a lot of attention here, and Bill Laws found himself in the midst of it.

"Emotions ran high," Ellen Laws said of the atmosphere within the church as well as in the community. "Bill had some long conferences with (a young man who was a member of the church) about his struggle with his conscience. When he finally went before the draft board, Bill went with him." Laws was angrily rebuked by the president of the draft board for "encouraging our youth to be traitors and draft dodgers." Ellen said that it was some time before her husband was able to discuss his thoughts on this with the draft board president. "Bill believed the church was more than ever needed in those angry days to be available to all its members, regardless of their opposing views, to assure them of God's love and grace through their most painful experiences."

It was a turbulent time, but Laws was a calming influence as he crisscrossed the country, visiting synods, presbyteries and churches, making what is believed to be 62 such stops, traveling as far as Seattle, San Francisco and Jacksonville. During that year, he was also part of a 60-member Protestant contingent that participated in a weeklong fact-finding consultation on the Paris Peace Talks in France.

One of Laws' major goals was to unify the northern and southern Presbyterian churches in the United States; they'd been split since the Civil War.

"I would like to travel in the South and visit the churches," he said in a June 12, 1970, article in The Republic. "I don't see myself as a flaming liberal, and I think I can make a contribution to unification."

Unification came in 1982, ending a 120-year split. Cal Brand Jr. was a commissioner at the General Assembly when reunification took place.

"That opportunity to vote for reunion ... that was really a payback to Bill," Brand said. "He was the pastor here when I decided I wanted to try seminary."

Brand wasn't the only person Laws inspired to go into seminary.

"He was so influential in my spiritual life," Lindemann said. "He urged not only me, but my brother, Tim, to consider the ministry. It took me a while to become a minister (I think I was 60 or 61), but I re-

---

"Bill believed the church was more than ever needed in those angry days to be available to all its members, regardless of their opposing views, to assure them of God's love and grace through their most painful experiences."

— Ellen Laws

member Dr. Laws saying to me one time, 'The Lord's got business with Skip Lindemann.'"

\*\*\*

During that year Laws' preaching caught the attention of a certain young California minister during a visit to the Pasadena Presbyterian Church.

"One hot and smoggy Sunday afternoon in the fall of 1970, I took my church youth group to a youth event," that minister recalled. "Bill Laws, the middle-aged pastor of a church in southern Indiana (of all places) … was the speaker. Seated in the balcony, the kids were restless and inattentive in the heat and heavy air as Dr. Laws rose to speak. However, his sonorous voice and engaging manner soon had them mesmerized, and I was pretty impressed myself."

That young minister? David Liddle, who seven years later came to First Presbyterian to serve as associate pastor before taking over as lead pastor in 1982.

\*\*\*

In 1975, as Laws contemplated his retirement, the congregation named his associate pastor, Warner Bailey, co-pastor. Of the many things Bailey noted in the way Laws did his job was the way he treated the church staff.

"Bill modeled a type of staff meeting that combined shared worship leadership and care for each other," Bailey said. "He said that the way the staff interacted was the most long-running example to the congregation of how we all should behave. I was astonished by the stellar cast of congregational leaders and their availability to share their skills and knowledge."

Bill Laws (right) chats with (from left) Waldo Harrison, Florence Hamilton, and Sarah Hunt.

"As a leader, Bill was a guy who had a great belief in process," Newlin said in a Dec. 6, 1985, story in The Republic. "He was a patient, low-key person. He didn't press people to move until they were ready to move. He knew getting the decision done in a right way was as important as getting it done."

In 1976 after 26 years as minister here, Laws resigned. He and Ellen moved to Keokuk, Iowa, where he had accepted a pastorate at Westminster United Presbyterian Church.

He'd left quite a big footprint in Columbus. He served on the boards of United Way, Bartholomew County Consolidated School Foundation, American Red Cross and Irwin Union Bank and Trust, and was

---

"Bill modeled a type of staff meeting that combined shared worship leadership and care for each other. He said that the way the staff interacted was the most long-running example to the congregation of how we all should behave."

— The Rev. Warner Bailey

a member of the Heritage Fund. He was also associated with Children Inc., Driftwood Valley Arts Council, Community Resources Center, Ministry for Texas Migrant Workers in the Columbus area and American Field Service.

He established the William R. Laws Scholarship Foundation, dedicated to higher education of African Americans in 1962. This developed following some informal discussions among Black residents the previous year in which they studied the current opportunities for the city's Black citizens. Their concern covered all areas, but their main concern became trying to increase the number of Black students moving on to educational opportunities beyond high school. The Laws Scholarship Foundation gave loans and grants to Black high school students for college or other advanced training. Later, the program was expanded to include all students. Early on, the program also helped in the recruitment of Black teachers, sponsored tutorial classes and tours, provided nursery school funding, and provided summer camp scholarships.[1]

Laws was so well thought of locally that the city of Columbus' Human Rights Commission named its annual human rights award for him.

Laws was also instrumental in the formation of the Ecumenical Assembly, spearheading its Equality Under the Law committee, and was the driving force behind the first community Good Friday service in Columbus. This assembly came about shortly after a large layoff in Columbus.

"He was concerned that there was a group of people who were newly unemployed," Newlin said years later. "He had a sense that something needed to be done. He led the community to get it done."

Meanwhile, the Louisville Presbyterian Seminary named a conference and retreat center for him and his wife. The $5.5 million William R. and Ellen Laws Lodge was completed in spring 2000. It included 49 guest rooms, offices, three classrooms and a chapel.[2]

\*\*\*

Saying his goodbyes to the congregation on Sunday, Feb. 28, 1976, Laws felt it was time for the parties to separate for some time. "In my judgment that is long enough, perhaps even too long. I do not want to overstay a significant ministry. A transplant will be both refreshing and challenging for me," he added, also saying he planned to return in five years to live the rest of his days in Columbus.

Laws was aware that the respect and attachment he'd earned might make it difficult for his successor, which was why he wanted "to create some emotional space between him and the congregation he had served with such love and effectiveness," Bailey said.

Laws also felt he was leaving the flock in quite capable hands.

Four years later Bill and Ellen Laws returned for good with Bill still performing some pastoral duties part time. The church received special permission from the Presbytery to name him pastor emeritus. His return, even part time, could have caused issues, but he never let that happen.

"He was sensitive to the boundary issues and ethical minefields involved in negotiating the relationship between current and former pastors of a congregation," Liddle recalled. When a congregant asked Laws to perform a wedding, for example, the former pastor gently reminded the couple that current pastors should be asked to officiate or to ask Laws to assist in conducting the service.

---

1 "Laws Foundation" *History of Bartholomew County Indiana Volume II 20th Century*, Bartholomew County Historical Society, 2003.
2 Blair, Brian. "Seminary lodge has Laws' name." *The Republic*. June 16, 1999.

His wife, Ellen, was soft-spoken, insightful and gracious, Liddle said. She was elected an elder and served on session for three years.

Bill Laws died on Dec. 5, 1985. His funeral drew a full house to the sanctuary, assembly room (now named for him) and church gymnasium with friends, family, community members and representatives from every level of the Presbyterian Church. Tributes to his life and legacy of his ministry poured in afterward, too.

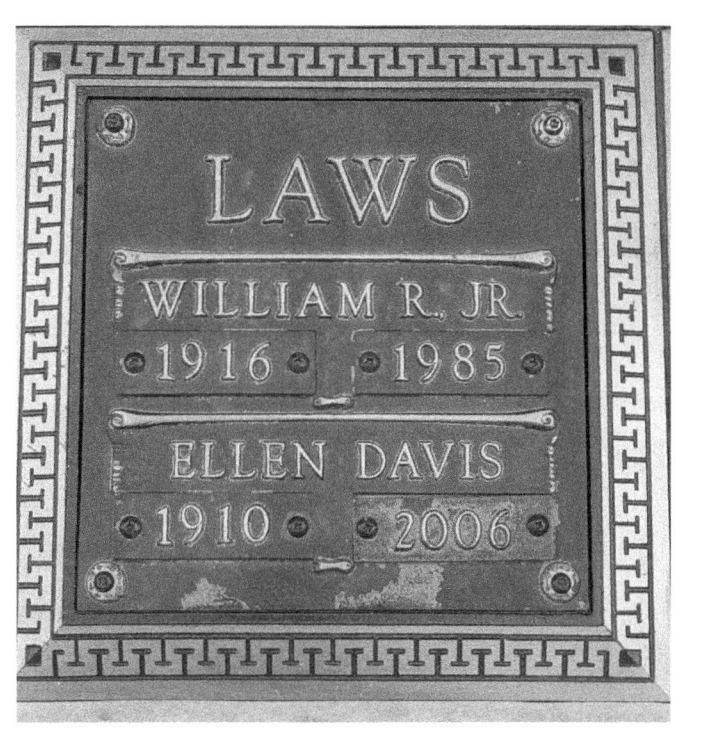

A story in *The Republic* the day after Laws passed away featured remembrances by those who knew him well. Among the quoted was the Rev. Charles Sims of Calvary Pentecostal Church.

"He was a catalyst for social justice in this community," said Sims, an African American pastor. "His efforts for equality will long be appreciated by me and my congregation."

Sims said Laws had the "courage to speak out when it was unpopular to do so" and hoped that the social consciousness Laws brought to Columbus would remain. He also said the William R. Laws Scholarship Foundation established by Laws "has been an asset for minorities and the poor of this community."

Bill and Ellen Laws are interred in the columbarium at First Presbyterian. // Photo by Paul J. Hoffman

Others gave the newspaper similar sentiments regarding Laws, perhaps none as respectful as those given by Miller.

"With equal compassion and extraordinary courage, he reminded the citizens of Columbus of their own weaknesses and shortcomings," he said. "He led in opening this community to all minorities. He was a champion of the poor and of everyone who was in any way excluded."

Miller went on to say that Laws understood young people and understood when he ought to take up their causes, as well as when to remind them of their responsibilities and obligations.

"Bill was not always a comfortable friend or pastor," Miller said. "He was instead a very model of the Christian faith and of Christian courage, quietly determined to pursue the right as he saw the right, without counting personal cost.

"Columbus will be for a very long time a better place because Bill Laws lived among us."

"In my time here, no one in this community has been more associated with causes to help the community," said Marilyn Hayes, who served for many years on the board of the Laws Foundation.

He and Ellen remain a part of First Presbyterian Church, both spiritually and physically, as they are interred in the church's columbarium.

# A Growing Congregation in a Growing Community

**When Bill Laws accepted** the call of the Columbus Presbyterian Church in 1950, the congregation numbered 573. Columbus was a growing town, having increased its population in the previous decade by 56.5 percent to 18,370 people.[1] Over the '50s and '60s, it would quickly grow to a small city of over 26,000 residents, with a suddenly diverse population.

The congregation grew with the community, greatly increasing the workload of the minister. By the late 1950s the congregation had more than 1,000 members, making it necessary to have two services each Sunday. The need for more clergy arose, and retired minister Dr. Jesse Tidball, who had been interim pastor before Laws was called, was hired as part-time assistant minister of visitation. Tidball, originally from Cincinnati, served pastorates in Illinois before moving to Madison in 1923, where he served the United Madison Presbyterian Church for 24 years. After spending 1950 to 1965 in Columbus, Tidball retired for good, moving to Tucson.[2]

Ed Wicklein, our first full-time assistant minister, was hired in 1959.

Sarah Hunt, second from left, leads a Christian education class at a fall retreat in 1952.

In 1959, Ed Wicklein came as our first full-time assistant minister, charged with the Christian education of the congregation. A Milwaukee native, Wicklein ended up pastoring seven Presbyterian churches around the country and Nepal, finally settling in New Mexico.[3] Wicklein, along with Sarah Hunt and Ken Hauser, gave adult literacy lessons to migrant workers at Golden Foundry who needed English lessons. Wicklein put together a special dictionary especially for these workers, according to Ellen Laws.

\*\*\*

---

1  "Indiana's Census 2020 Redistricting Data Dashboard." Census.gov. Archived from the original on July 25, 2021. Retrieved Oct. 3, 2021.
2  *The (Columbus) Republic,* April 10, 1970.
3  *St. Louis Post-Dispatch*, Aug. 9, 2017.

# 200 YEARS of FIRST PRESBYTERIAN CHURCH of COLUMBUS, INDIANA

With the leadership of Lawrence E. Reeves, the congregation established the Presbyterian Foundation (now called the First Presbyterian Church Foundation) in 1952 for the purpose of receiving bequests, memorials and other gifts and expending such funds to promote religious, educational and charitable purposes of the congregation. Reeves, a businessman and longtime civic leader, was elected first president of the organization. He also served on the Columbus School Board, earned the chamber's community service award in 1958, was the 9th District Democratic chairman for years, chairman of the board of the Scott County State Bank for nearly 30 years, and in his earlier days taught school. [4]

The foundation never intended to assume the responsibility of financing budgetary items but has been instrumental many times in helping the congregation meet unexpected, unbudgeted expenses, such as boiler replacement and repairs to the building. The foundation has assisted with many diverse projects, just some of which were:

- A new playground for the church.

- The establishment of the Lincoln-Central Neighborhood Family Center in 1994.

- The Friends of Calnali building project in Mexico in 2001.

- Sending the church's preschool staff to national educational conferences.

***

Education has long been paramount with Presbyterians, both nationally and in Columbus. On Jan. 11, 1954, the church opened the first weekday preschool (called a nursery school at the time) in town with 25 children enrolled. There were no restrictions on religious or other background, and there still aren't today. The church's preschool parents' study group,

First Presbyterian opened the first weekday preschool in Columbus in January 1954, at first called a nursery school. It was, and still is, open to all children regardless of faith. Staff members in 1955 were, from top: Florence Hamilton, director; Bernice Collins, nurse; Alice Schwab, teacher. Bottom photo: preschoolers visit an Air Force airplane at the Columbus airport.

---
4 *The Evening Republican*, Feb. 17, 1966.

When the school bell rings this fall, it also will ring for the "small fry" of the community. The Presbyterian nursery school opens again on Monday, Sept. 13, in the kindergarten room.

The week-day nursery school was a new idea in this community and was put into practice here last year after the realization of the need for such a group had formulated in a pre-school parent study group which met monthly at the Presbyterian church.

The pre-school study group dates back four years and was first formulated by Mrs. Ted George. There are now approximately 60 members in this group.

There are no restrictions of religion or other background for those who desire to attend the nursery, and it is operated on a non-profit basis.

The nursery school is a supplement to, not a substitute for, the home.

The little ones will be given contact with living things, such as babies, seeds, small animals, through which they may learn to realize the marvel of growth and the abundance of beauty and design in the world of nature.

They will given the opportunity to learn that there is joy in sharing and in personal achievement as well as in singing, dancing and drawing.

— The Evening Republican // Sept. 1, 1954

"It (preschool) sets the standard."

— The Rev. Felipe N. Martinez

under the direction of Margaret George, organized the school. Classes for ages 3½ to 6 (or whenever they were eligible for public school kindergarten) were held Mondays, Wednesdays and Fridays from 9 to 11 a.m. Mary Jo Cummins, a former kindergarten teacher in Columbus, was the first teacher, while Mary Jones was the business manager and Bernice Collins the nurse.[5] George and Jones were credited with the bulk of the work in setting up the school.

The program was in such demand that at the beginning of March a second class was added on Tuesday and Thursday mornings. Florence Hamilton taught this class, bringing the total enrollment to 50 children. By the start of the fall 1954 semester, the staff consisted of five women, with four more serving on the nursery school policy committee. Pre-care and after-care were added much later.

"It sets the standard," said current pastor, the Rev. Dr. Felipe Martinez, of the preschool.

It has been called by various names over the years:

- Presbyterian Nursery School, opened in 1954
- Presbyterian Pre-School Center, 1956
- First United Presbyterian Pre-School Center, 1963
- First Presbyterian Preschool [6]

In the 70 years since, Alice Schwab, Nancy Sawin, Becky Monroe, Barbara Newton and April Hemmerlein have served as directors, and enrollment has reached 180. Newton served for 27 of those years.

5 *The Evening Republican*, Jan. 18, 1954.
6 Corbit, Dana. "Teaching toddlers." *The Republic*, February 16, 1990.

In the 1960s, Presbyterians went a step further. As more women entered the workforce, good child care became more difficult to find, and a child care center was opened in the church, meeting in the basement and some adult classrooms. This eventually became Children Inc., which had a center at the church until 2001, when it consolidated with other similar programs and has been located at 715 McClure Road ever since.

In a column discussing Children Inc.'s move, long-time local journalist Harry McCawley stated, "Nothing against the McClure Road center or any of the other operations around town, but for a lot of people those rooms at First Presbyterian educational center WERE child care in Columbus. In one respect, First Presbyterian was where child care as we know it began here."[7]

With all these programs going on at the church, it became apparent more room was needed. In 1964, the Assembly Room was changed dramatically. A second floor was put in, eliminating the balcony that had surrounded it. The tops of the tall windows on the south side of the room were then cut off from the view from the first floor. Upstairs, offices and a hallway were built on the south side, with a library/meeting room in the center. There were now eight classrooms upstairs, rather than four. Construction was done by Dunlap Construction.[8]

\*\*\*

In October 1958 the church changed its name from First Presbyterian Church to First United Presbyterian Church following the merger of the Presbyterian Church in the U.S.A. and the United Presbyterian Church the previous spring.[9]

\*\*\*

After the city's only Black barber, Grant U. Smith, the son of former slaves, retired in his early 90s and closed his shop in the early 1960s, no white barbers here would cut Black men's hair. That meant Black men were forced to drive long distances for a professional haircut. The first white barber in Columbus to accept Black customers was a member of First Presbyterian, Luell Cook, whose motivation to do so was prompted by his relationship to Benjamin "Mickey" King, an African American on the Human Rights Commission and a county hospital microbiologist who also attended First Presbyterian.

Cook told a reporter after a Mayor's Commission on Human Rights Relations meeting in May 1964 that he "simply couldn't stand going to church and seeing Mr. King there and hearing sermons on brotherhood while running a shop closed to Negroes. I decided that if I was enough of a Christian to go to church, I should be enough of a Christian to practice my religion at work." Cook said he had lost some customers to his decision, "but most of my customers couldn't care less. Most of them didn't even know Negroes couldn't get their hair cut in Columbus, and they thought it awful they had to drive to Indianapolis or Shelbyville for a barber."[10]

Elizabeth "Lib" Boyles, also a member of First Presbyterian, was the first to open her restaurant – Lib's

> "I decided that if I was enough of a Christian to go to church, I should be enough of a Christian to practice my religion at work."
>
> — Luell Cook, the first white barber in Columbus to accept African American men as customers.

---

7  *The Republic*, July 24, 2001.
8  "Remodel church interior." *The Republic,* Dec. 5, 1964.
9  "Church changes name." *The Republic,* October 23, 1958.
10  Rutherford, John. "This barber does cut Negroes' hair." *The Evening Republican,* May 21, 1964.

# 200 YEARS of FIRST PRESBYTERIAN CHURCH of COLUMBUS, INDIANA

Clockwise from top left: senior high fellowship, 1954; first- through third-grade Sunday school class; young women attend church school, 1955; kindergartners portrayed sheep and shepherds in the lost sheep story from the Bible during the summer of 1947; kindergartners check out a model of the church, 1953.

Nook at 534 Washington St. – to Black diners. Some other restaurants would allow Black people in but made them sit in a special section. Boyles' place was open to Blacks from the mid-1950s on. Had jazz great Louis Armstrong walked into Lib's Nook in 1957 instead of the other two eateries he tried to enter around Third Street, he'd have been served instead of turned away, Boyles' daughter, Charlotte Aldenhagen, said years later. Armstrong was in town as a guest of the Columbus Jaycees to perform in the highly successful Auditorium Series at Columbus High School's Memorial Gym.[11]

\*\*\*

The federal Fair Housing Act was first passed in 1968, though Indiana had similar laws prior to this. Violations of the law weren't always reported, and when they were, they weren't always enforced.

Larry Long, a member of the 150th anniversary committee, found out first-hand what African Americans faced when trying to find housing in Columbus. While working at Golden Foundry as a teen in the summers of 1962 and 1963, he worked with mainly African Americans. Since the high school here had no Blacks, Long wondered where the Black men lived who worked there.

The answer he got was, "Don't you know that we can't buy homes in Bartholomew County? It is redlined, and we all live in North Vernon and Vernon."

In Columbus, Bill Laws and J. Irwin Miller spearheaded an effort to get Columbus to approve and enforce open housing. Dunlap and Co. owned the only two standalone apartment buildings in the city, one on Washington Street and one near the middle school; neither allowed Black residents until pressure came to comply.

Miller, president of Irwin Union Bank and Trust Co. and Cummins Engine Co., was recruiting African Americans to work in Columbus during this time. He'd long been involved in civic projects. So when Cummins' African American employees were denied occupancy to these apartments based on their skin color, Miller said he would no longer house any employees, regardless of color, in those buildings if they were "closed," meaning off limits to Blacks.

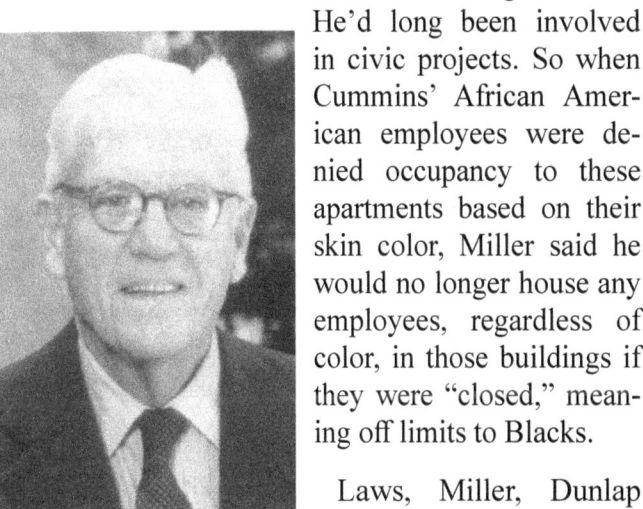

Laws, Miller, Dunlap owners Jerry and Isabel Dunlap and Calvert Brand, a First Presbyterian member who was managing the apartment buildings at the time, worked together until the Dunlap policy changed, Brand's son, Cal Brand Jr., said.

"It was very segregated in the '60s," Long said. "Both Bill Laws and Irwin Miller were at work trying to create a better world."

\*\*\*

Also during this period, church members like Isabel Ritter, Mickey and Ann King, and Susie Jones, to name only a few, took the lead in adult literacy, minority tutoring programs and a migrant ministry. The county migrant ministry provided services to some of the 30,000 migrant workers who annually came to Indiana

*Calvert Brand, left, was instrumental in helping Cummins executive J. Irwin Miller, right, and Bill Laws achieve open housing in Columbus.*

---
11  McCawley, Harry. "Local cook served meals but withheld the bigotry." *The Republic*, Jan. 25, 2001.

Members of First Presbyterian play with children of migrant families in the early 1960s at a farm south of Columbus.

Fairlawn Presbyterian started conducting services on the northeast side of town in the fall of 1962 with 46 families from First Presbyterian. // Paul J. Hoffman

to harvest produce as well as to trim Christmas trees. Social workers provided recreation for children and enrolled them in schools and English lessons and offered legal assistance.[12] Many of the migrants worked at the Donald Thompson farm near Waynesville, south of Columbus, where roughly 15 migrant families lived in converted semi-trailers for three months each year.[13]

\*\*\*

By the end of the 1950s, the city of Columbus had grown to the north and east. Some downtown churches had moved into those areas. Retail establishments, too, were beginning to leave downtown for shopping centers to the northeast. Presbyterians considered the need to serve the growing northeast side. Should they, too, move to that area?

The congregation decided to remain a downtown church but to colonize a new Presbyterian church, which was to become Fairlawn Presbyterian. In 1961, the downtown congregation received a gift of seven acres at the corner of Walnut Drive and State Road 46 (now 25th Street and Fairlawn Drive) by Jerald and Maxine Dunlap, Evans and Isabel Dunlap, Bruce and Phyllis Warren, and Calvert and Betty Brand. The church unanimously approved the move at an annual congregational dinner on Oct. 11. The decision culminated more than a year of study.[14]

"The Presbyterian Church was encouraging churches to move from downtown," Ben Bush said. "(By starting Fairlawn), we stayed downtown, but what we did complied with the national request."

Donald M. Brower, a Wisconsin native and pastor at Springhill Presbyterian Church near Greensburg, was called as organizing pastor of the as-yet-unnamed church.[15] The first service was conducted on Oct. 4, 1962, with 46 charter families that had withdrawn from First Presbyterian. Laws preached and conducted Communion that morning. The church building was a two-story colonial structure with white col-

---

12 "Church Women United aids Indiana's Migrant Workers." *The Republic*, Jan. 27, 1968.
13 "Migrant worker camp gets okay." *The Republic*. May 31, 1962.
14 "Site is given for 2nd church." *The Evening Republican*, Oct. 12, 1961.
15 "Church selects pastor." *The Evening Republican*, Oct. 3, 1962.

umns and a peaked roof and a color scheme of blue and white. It was built with five Sunday school rooms in the basement. The sanctuary could accommodate up to 160 people, and the music was supplied by electric organ. The church donated $5,000 for landscaping, church supplies and sanctuary equipment.[16] The new church was officially dubbed Fairlawn United Presbyterian Church in early March 1963.

Once it was organized and going strong, some families who started it returned to First Presbyterian.

\*\*\*

Ed Wicklein resigned as assistant minister in September 1964 and moved to Bay City, Michigan.[17] He was replaced by I. Barnett Shepherd, a native of Mississippi who was later named associate minister. Shepherd came to Columbus from St. Stephen Presbyterian Church in Birmingham, Alabama.[18] He left in 1968, obtained a degree in art history and taught in that field in Florida before writing a book, "Sailors' Snug Harbor: 1801-1976," about a hospital and home for retired sailors on Staten Island.[19]

The Rev. Jerry Kerns was associate minister here from 1968-1972.

Jerry Kerns was associate minister from 1968 to 1972. It was Kerns who took over much of the local ministerial work while Bill Laws served as moderator in 1970.

\*\*\*

Ramon (Ray) Hass was hired as our first full-time minister of music in June 1961, replacing Ted Hunt, who had accepted the same position at St. Paul's Episcopal Church in the city. An Iowa native who went to Coe College and taught music in the Cedar Rapids schools before spending two years in the Army, Hass then obtained a master's degree in sacred music from Union Theological Seminary in New York City. While a student there, he also served as organist and choir director at Sunset Park Methodist Church in Brooklyn.[20]

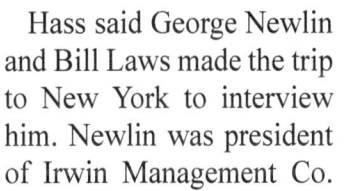

Hass said George Newlin and Bill Laws made the trip to New York to interview him. Newlin was president of Irwin Management Co. at the time, and his brother-in-law was a teacher at a seminary Hass had attended. One of the reasons he was drawn to First Presbyterian was Laws' concern with social justice issues, especially racial issues, at the time.

Ray Hass was hired as minister of music in 1961. He oversaw the purchase of new organs in 1965 and 1995, retiring in 2001.

Hass wasn't here long before the decision to purchase a new organ was made. When he arrived, the congregation was using a small Kimball organ of 10

---

16 "Presbyterian group to meet in new church Sunday." The Evening Republican, Oct. 6, 1962.
17 "Rev. Wicklein to leave church here." The Evening Republican, June 22, 1964.
18 "New assistant pastor at Presbyterian church." The Evening Republican, Sept. 4, 1965.
19 Jean Prather, "Historic Snug Harbor home cared for 'decrepit sailors.'" The Republic, Sept. 14, 1979.
20 "New minister of music will begin duties here." The Evening Republican, May 31, 1961.

# 200 YEARS of FIRST PRESBYTERIAN CHURCH of COLUMBUS, INDIANA

Clockwise from top left: Cub Scouts compete in the Pinewood Derby, 1962; Christmas play, 1960; honoring graduates in 1963; the intermediate choir, 1962; what the 1968 data showed a typical member of First Presbyterian to be.

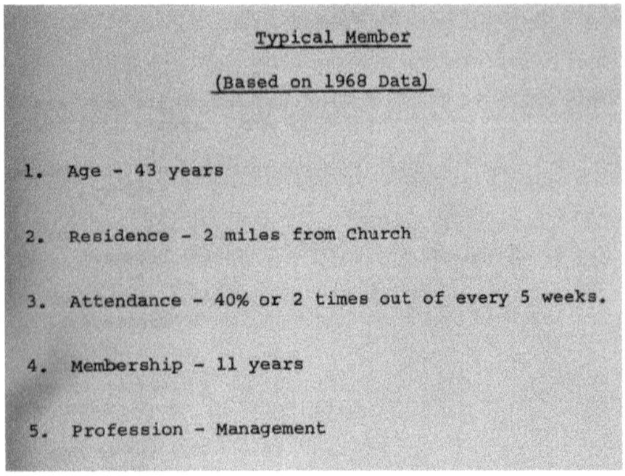

```
                Typical Member
              (Based on 1968 Data)


    1.  Age - 43 years

    2.  Residence - 2 miles from Church

    3.  Attendance - 40% or 2 times out of every 5 weeks.

    4.  Membership - 11 years

    5.  Profession - Management
```

76

# 200 YEARS of FIRST PRESBYTERIAN CHURCH of COLUMBUS, INDIANA

The adult choir, under the direction of Ramon (Ray) Hass, as pictured in the 1972 First Presbyterian Church directory.

ranks (61 keys) that had been in use since 1941[21][22]. In 1965, the church purchased a Reuter, which had 22 ranks. Today's organ, bought in 1995, has 47 ranks.

The dedication service of the Reuter was held Feb. 28, 1965, climaxing nearly three years of planning and preparation, which was custom-built by the Reuter Pipe Organ Co. of Lawrence, Kansas. The instrument had 1,257 pipes controlled by 27 stops. It was purchased by members and friends of the congregation who matched a challenge gift by Paul and Eva Reeves. The previous organ, a gift from the Frederick Donner family, was sold to Jonesville Lutheran Church.[23]

For many years, Hass oversaw four choirs: adult, youth (Grades 7-12), junior (Grades 4-6) and primary (Grades 1-3). By the time he retired, the interest in the youth choir had dwindled.

He was a co-founder of an adult church choir festival in town, which lasted six to seven years in the 1970s. Five churches were involved: First United Methodist, First Presbyterian, First Baptist, North Christian and First Christian. He also helped start a youth festival choir in the same era.

Hass specifically recalls a harrowing experience in the late '70s or early '80s directing choirs in the singing of Christmas carols at The Commons downtown during the Festival of Trees, the precursor to today's Festival of Lights. Back then, there was a balcony at The Commons, and the choir members in the balcony couldn't see Hass on the floor below. So he climbed to the top of a 20-foot ladder, directing from there.

"I certainly feared for my life," he said. "I must have directed from memory. I never got on that ladder again."

In 1966, Hass became a certified church worker and took on duties beyond the music program of the church. He stayed for 40 years before retiring as music director in 2001. He still sings in the choir on occasion.

\*\*\*

Beginning in the late 1960s, the turmoil of the Vietnam War that affected the whole country touched the congregation, too. Some supported the war effort; others opposed it. Families with sons serving in the war zone deeply resented peace petitions that were placed in the church by an outside group. It was a stressful time for the congregation.

---

21 Bicknell, Stephen. "Organ construction." *The Cambridge Companion to the Organ,* pp. 20. Cambridge University Press (1999). A rank is a set of pipes of the same timbre but multiple pitches (one for each note on the keyboard), which is mounted (usually vertically) onto a windchest.
22 "Presbyterian church to dedicate organ Sunday." *The Evening Republican*, Feb. 27, 1965.
23 Ibid.

The so-called "hippie" movement, which coincided to some degree with American involvement in Vietnam, touched many young people with its anti-establishment, distrust-of-authority message.

The congregation and the hippies cooperated in a venture in the late 1960s. The church had owned the old Vetter apartment house at 725 Franklin St., just to the north of the church, with plans to raze it and put in a parking lot. But before that took place, the vacant house was turned into a coffeehouse named One Step Down, a teen entertainment center for Grades 10 and older where members of the congregation served as chaperones. This center, opened on June 15, 1967, was started and run mainly by youth groups from First Presbyterian, First Methodist and Fairlawn Presbyterian, as well as other youths in the community. Nancy Gronning, youth education director at First Methodist, and the Rev. I. Barnett Shepherd of First Presbyterian, were key chaperones. The coffeehouse was open at least once a week and featured folk music and poetry readings. Longtime FPC member Danny Clark helped paint the coffeehouse, and he and his band mates played music there. Coffee and soda pop were sold. There was no admission charge, but free-will offerings were accepted.[24]

The coffeehouse eventually became controversial with some church members and the police. An upside-down American flag, universal symbol of distress, painted on a wall may have been the last straw, something the FBI investigated. Or it may have been a burst water pipe, which did considerable damage. Or it may have just been a waning interest, as the Rev. Jerry Kerns said. Whichever it was, the place closed in the fall of 1968.

Five months later, the Pacific Experience coffeehouse replaced it in the same building, though significantly upgraded, and with a new purpose. Pacific Experience was based more on teens being involved than being entertained. Programs each Saturday night were to be thought-provoking and featured experimental art films, underground movies, folk singers and discussions with community leaders.[25]

Pacific Experience lasted about 18 months; the house was razed in 1971 and a parking lot put in.

\*\*\*

Despite the uneasiness of the times, the church continued to be on the leading edge of ministry to the community. Love Chapel, a small church in East Columbus, had long been under the joint support of several churches, as had the FISH program, providing food for needy families. Presbyterian efforts for these two programs were spearheaded by Willard "Chick" Shull and Cal Wright.

Originally called Love's Chapel Separate Baptist Church and then Love's Chapel Mission, it opened at 703 Ross St. in 1949. Love Chapel had moved to Center Street by 1952. It's been there ever since and is a ministry of the Ecumenical Assembly of Bartholomew County Churches. Today, Love Chapel is a nonprofit charitable organization, providing access to food, shelter and financial assistance. Its services are for everyone.[26] Members Jeff Crump and Sarah Sanders are currently on the board.

Longtime member Danny Clark played music at One Step Down, the coffeehouse just north of the church, in the late 1960s.

---
24 "New coffeehouse opening tonight." *The Republic*, June 15, 1967.
25 "Coffeehouse reopens with new name and new purpose." *The Republic*, March 22, 1969.
26 "About us," https://columbuslovechapel.com

# 200 YEARS of FIRST PRESBYTERIAN CHURCH of COLUMBUS, INDIANA

The FISH (Friend, I Shall Help!) program is a nationwide organization. Member churches contributed money and food. In 1976, the effort in Columbus had a 24-hour emergency answering service and contributed 32 bags of food to needy families each month.[27]

For a time, the congregation welcomed students from Indiana University who had come here from abroad. The students and their families stayed with church families.

First Presbyterian also arranged for several years to host a bus load of departing American Field Service students over the July 4th weekend. Then, in 1960-61, we hosted our first year-long student. Many other students followed, and many of our students also spent a year abroad.

\*\*\*

Several members of First Presbyterian helped found the Columbus Peace Education Fellowship on Oct. 2, 1967. Laws invited to his home people interested in peace for Vietnam to meet with Carl Landes of the American Friends Service committee. Now called the Columbus Peace Fellowship, original members included Ray Hass, Ted and Sarah Hunt, Winifred Lindemann, William Lion, Joan Riffle and Thelma Triplett. The focus of the group was the Vietnam War until 1975, at which time other peace initiatives filled the docket.[28]

\*\*\*

In the late 1960s, an interdenominational study group "stirred by an urgent conviction that Christians need to think and act together in this crisis-filled world" was

> In the late 1960s, an interdenominational study group "stirred by an urgent conviction that Christians need to think and act together in this crisis-filled world" was instrumental in the formation of the Ecumenical Assembly of Bartholomew County Churches.

instrumental in the formation of the Ecumenical Assembly of Bartholomew County Churches. A group of clergy and lay people met three times in 1967 with the first meeting in March. Out of that came the Ecumenical Assembly. Representatives from nine member churches met in the fall of 1968 to elect a board of directors, who in turn elected officers for the year. John Thomas of First United Presbyterian, an attorney at Arvin Industries, was one of the first officers. The work was to be carried out by two committees: the social action committee, which developed and implemented programs for Christian responses to community social needs; and the communications committee, which developed and implemented programs for intercommunication on spiritual matters among its members.[29]

This group eventually took over the administration of the FISH and Emergency Assistance programs, with Love Chapel as its base.

Another example of different faiths working together came in 1975, when St. Bartholomew Catholic Church was undergoing a complete remodeling. That congregation worshipped in the First Presbyterian sanctuary early each Sunday morning during the construction period. This was considered a bold move on the part of both congregations.

\*\*\*

First Presbyterian has a history of helping refugees.

In 1962, the congregation accepted sponsorship of Manuel Martinez, his wife and children ages 11 and 7, a family of refugees from Communist Cuba. This

---

27 "Assembly offers report for '76." *The Republic*, Feb. 5, 1977.
28 "Columbus Peace Fellowship has 10th anniversary." *The Republic*, Sept. 29, 1977.
29 Knicely, Donna. "Ecumenical church group seeks 'oneness in Christ.'" *The Republic*, Nov. 22, 1968.

was part of a Freedom Flight initiative, where sponsors were sought for five Cuban families scheduled to make their homes here. Prospective employers were also contacted ahead of time. At the time, many Cuban refugees were making their way to Miami, Florida, from the Fidel Castro-led island, with some planning to move on elsewhere. The cost to sponsor a family was approximately $300.[30]

First United Presbyterian was one of five sponsoring churches in the local Cuban Refugee Relocation organization. Four families and a single man arrived here on Oct. 5. Martinez, 35, spoke and read English well when he arrived. He was an electrician with experience as a lineman.[31] He began work almost immediately at Bartholomew County REMC. Housing and furnishings had been secured ahead of time, and the children all started school the following Monday.

Arriving here ended a six-month trip since Martinez left his homeland, about which he said to a local reporter, "We hope someday to see our country free. People are always looking over their shoulder to see if anyone is following them or listening to them." He explained how someone like Castro could come to power: "When somebody says he wants to help you, sometimes you believe him. You don't find out he was lying until later, when he stabs you in the back." The refugees could have stayed in Miami and received government support, but "we want to make it on our own now," he added.[32]

Sakoune Phommarath, right, his wife, Keooudone, left, and their two children arrived in Columbus in 1980 after fleeing the Communist regime in Laos. Members of First Presbyterian helped get the family situated here.

Later, the church sponsored the Sakoune Phommarath family from Laos, as well as the Nguyen family and Kim Hanh Tran and her sons, both families from Vietnam. The Phommarath family arrived in spring 1980 through the Church World Support agency. Sakoune and his wife, Keooudone, had two young children. Like the Martinez family nearly two decades prior, Sakoune decided to leave Laos due to Communism. The family sold personal items to raise money to leave the country in secret. He and another

---

"When somebody says he wants to help you, sometimes you believe him. You don't find out he was lying until later, when he stabs you in the back."

— Manuel Martinez, Cuban refugee on why he and his family fled Fidel Castro-governed Cuba in 1962

---

30 "Seek job for refugees." *The Republic*, May 18, 1962.
31 "Public support is asked for new Cuban families." *The Republic*, Oct. 2, 1962.
32 Nance, Lee, "Cuban families are grateful." *The Republic*, Oct. 8, 1962.

man swam alongside the boat carrying their families across the Mekong River to Thailand, staying in a church camp there for 10 months before coming to the United States. Sakoune got a job at Human Services Inc. [33]

Eight members of the Nguyen Quang Du family arrived in Columbus from Pennsylvania in July 1975 with the assistance of the Kelly Mather family. The Nguyens had fled Saigon by boat as the North Vietnamese were taking over the city. The father, Du, was part of two refugee moves. His family had also fled from North Vietnam to South Vietnam in 1954 when he was 10 years old.[34]

Kim Hanh Tran followed her brother, Trung Vimh Tran, to Columbus. He arrived in 1975; she in 1990. A celebrated singer and photographer, Kim was also a flight attendant before she became a real estate agent in Columbus. She died in 2010.

All these families became American citizens.

***

This era had a major impact on all denominations. The young people who had rebelled against the authority of the church, the teachings of the church or perhaps their parents' insistence on church attendance stayed away when they became adults. Membership began to dwindle. In 1970, the congregation numbered 741.

First Presbyterian has been an avid supporter of Camp Pyoca in Jackson County. The camp, originally called Presbyterian Youth Camp of Brownstown, Indiana, has been in operation since 1950, when the Synod of Indiana acquired the land. The camp now operates independently, but remains aligned with the Presbyterian Church (USA). Top: The chapel at Camp Pyoca. Above: A group of campers from First Presbyterian.

---

33 Hailey, Lynn, "For Laotian family here, it's most treasured Christmas gift." *The Republic*, Dec. 24, 1980.
34 Carlson, Jon, "Refugee family begins job of adjusting." *The Republic*, July 2, 1975.

# A Major Building Project and Our First Female Ministers

**At the end of the 1960s** and the start of the 1970s, girls who were married were not allowed to continue their high school education, let alone unmarried pregnant girls. The church helped start a program to allow young mothers and mothers-to-be to finish their education, giving both meeting space and some financial assistance. After years of planning by concerned citizens, spearheaded by Jean Turpin, the Young Mothers Educational Development (Y-MED) program started in 1972, meeting in three rooms of the First Presbyterian education building.

Following the approval of a $32,800 grant from the Irwin-Miller-Sweeney Foundation to fund the first year of the school, members of the coordinating board hired a director. Academic subjects were taught each weekday, and a variety of non-academic classes – such as prenatal care, group therapy and guest speakers – were also taught. Three teachers approved by the Bartholomew Consolidated School Corp. were hired: Joyce Nottingham, Mary Kay Coachys and Gail Lyons.[1] The goal was to keep the girls earning credits accepted by the BCSC board and return them to school following their pregnancies.[2]

> The church helped start a program to allow young mothers and mothers-to-be to finish their education, giving both meeting space and some financial assistance.

The program later included students from the Flat Rock-Hawcreek School Corp., then changed its name to Route 21 in 2010. For a while, the program was supported through the United Way of Bartholomew County, then it became affiliated with Human Services Inc.[3] It was still going in the mid-2010s.

\*\*\*

The Child Care Clinic and the Emergency Assistance Fund were started with the leadership of Presbyterians, including Bob Aldenhagen and Effie Miller, as well as other churches. Miller was church secretary for 17 years. A mobile child care clinic, a combined effort of the Ecumenical Assembly of Bartholomew County Churches, opened on July 1, 1971. The clinic, which operated out of a van, provided preventive health care for preschool chil-

Longtime secretary Effie Miller was one of the key people involved in starting the Child Care and Emergency Fund in the county.

---

1  *The Republic*, Feb. 1, 1972.
2  *The Republic*, Jan. 29, 1972.
3  *The Republic*, Jan. 8, 2014.

dren who could not afford the services of a physician, lived in more remote areas of the county and were not covered by other assistance programs. Fees were set according to the ability to pay. The 36-foot-long van had been reconfigured from a 1958 U.S. Postal Service bus and had two exam rooms and a reception area. The clinic was supported by donations from local churches and individuals.[4] By 1976, there were two monthly clinics at Love Chapel and a bi-monthly one at Taylorsville. In that year, the clinic had hired a part-time coordinator, Linda Martin, conducted 266 examinations and given 621 immunizations.[5]

The Emergency Assistance Fund saw four churches split duties on administering funds in 1976. First Presbyterian was one of those churches. A caseload of 293 people was seen during its first 12 months.[6]

\*\*\*

The church celebrated its 150th anniversary in 1974 with three consecutive worship services starting on June 30. A special wreath laying service was held on the Wednesday prior to that service, when members laid a wreath at the grave of Joseph Hart in Garland Brook Cemetery.

A napkin from the 150th anniversary celebration on July 7, 1974.

The theme for the first celebratory service was "Our First 150 Years – Review and Appreciation." Ross Crump, an elder in the church and the son of a pioneer family, recounted some of the church's early struggles.

The theme for the second service, held on July 7, was "Our 150th Birthday Party." Plans included worship, fun, involvement of children, and a general celebration of family.

The final Sunday celebration, on July 14, was themed, "Our Next 150 Years: Fancy and Faithfulness." Laws used that day to discuss such issues as what the church had to look forward to, what do members want to give their children, and what can members do now to provide a rich heritage for future generations. Dr. William Birenbaum, president of Staten Island Community College, was the guest speaker at that service.

Ross Crump spoke at the 150th anniversary celebration. He was an elder, a descendant of one of Columbus' pioneer families and a historian.

Invitees included descendants of founding members, former pastors and church members, and members of the community.[7]

\*\*\*

In 1973, the church called Warner Bailey as associate minister. Two years later, he was named co-pastor with Bill Laws. Bailey took over as pastor, and he was joined on the staff by David Liddle, who became associate pastor in 1977.

Bailey had been professor of religion and philosophy at Franklin College for three years. A native Texan, he graduated from Texas Christian University in Dallas summa cum laude and received a

---

4 "Mobile child care clinic to open here July 1." *The Republic*, May 7, 1971.
5 "Assembly offers report for '76." *The Republic*, Feb. 5, 1977.
6 Ibid.
7 "Church marks Sesquicentennial." *The Republic*, June 29, 1974.

Bachelor of Divinity degree at Austin (Texas) Theological Seminary. He earned his doctorate degree in Old Testament studies at Yale University. He was called to the church here in February 1973, but his installation was delayed until the Franklin College semester ended.[8]

He had known Bill Laws since he first arrived in Franklin in 1970 when a mutual friend suggested he make himself known to Laws. He did, and that started a relationship that led to Laws asking Bailey to join him on staff.

Bailey, a bright man with a loud, booming laugh, was a good administrator and the guiding force in the establishment of a shelter for battered and abused women, of which he was one of the first board members. Organized in June 1979 as a collaboration between the Women's Center of Columbus, Quinco Consulting and the Salvation Army, it became known as The Columbus Regional Shelter for Victims of Domestic Violence Inc. Funding came from the Indiana Office of Social Services through a Title XX contract and from local foundations, businesses and individuals.[9]

Though the official name still stands, the center has been known as Turning Point for more than 40 years. In June 1981, the group chose Turning Point because "we wanted a greeting that meant something but wasn't as cumbersome as our official title," according to Barbara Raye, then the shelter director. Later that year, Turning Point, which had operated in multiple locations, opened a location at 745 Washington St.[10] It now has a 25-bed facility at 1531 13th St.

"Getting a shelter here was a real source of personal satisfaction," Bailey said. "We had a tough assignment because we met with such resistance, but the shelter was much needed."[11]

During his term at First Presbyterian, Bailey was appointed to the former North American Council of the World Alliance of Reformed Churches and was the featured lecturer at a national gathering on stewardship. Meanwhile, he advocated for the Children's

*Warner Bailey*

---

"Getting a (women's) shelter here was a real source of personal satisfaction. We had a tough assignment because we met with such resistance, but the shelter was much needed."

Warner Bailey

---

8 "Presbyterians to welcome Bailey." *The Republic*, June 6, 1973.
9 "Shelter responsibilities change hands." *The Republic*, Feb. 16, 1981.
10 "New name selected for domestic aid program." *The Republic*, June 23, 1981.
11 "Farewell: Warner Bailey accepts new pastorate in Texas." *The Republic*, Jan. 19, 1982.

The Rev. Warner Bailey, left, with his wife, Mary, and Jacquie Franz.

Home, helping to identify and retain Phil Wasmuth as alcohol and drug counselor for Bartholomew Consolidated School Corp., and was a member of several community organizations, serving on the boards of many of them. He oversaw the expansion of the nurture programs at First Presbyterian and contributed to its long-range planning.[12]

Among his other accomplishments here was increasing stewardship. He and the congregation were so successful at increasing our benevolence each year that they were asked to share the story of it with the denomination through a bulletin insert created by the General Assembly, he said.

Some of his happiest and most productive times at First Presbyterian were spent in Summer's Inn, a weekly Sunday afternoon gathering for small worship, intergenerational learning and bonding over a picnic.

"While we asked members of the congregation to sign up, we intentionally invited families who had not yet joined," he said, "and every one of those families eventually became members."

Bailey, who sometimes played autoharp during children's sermons, also enjoyed the Christmas Eve services, when children dressed up as Nativity characters. A large youth group during that time took trips to Chicago and Appalachia.

"They were mostly boys, and so our daughter began bringing her girlfriends," Bailey recalled.

Bailey left in early 1982 to become pastor and head of staff at the 1,300-member Ridglea Presbyterian Church in Fort Worth, Texas. He is still in Fort Worth with his wife, Mary.

\*\*\*

Men's and women's support groups sprang up during this time. Longtime member Sherry Stark recalled Bill Laws attended the women's group at first. "About one or two meetings in, as much as we loved him, we told him this is a women's support group and he didn't need to come," she said. He respected their wishes. Six of the early members still meet once a year now.

The first women's support group started during the end of Bill Laws' time as minister here. Some of the early members are pictured in 2006: Lynn Lucas, Janet Sharpe, Marilyn Metzler, Elizabeth Witte, Carolyn Seltzer and Sherry Stark.

---
12  Ibid.

# 200 YEARS of FIRST PRESBYTERIAN CHURCH of COLUMBUS, INDIANA

Photos from the 1972 member directory

"We shared our struggles with an air of confidentiality," Stark said, adding that at some point, others were invited to join. "It taught us so much about faith, trust and support.

Similarly, the men's group has survived. It was started by the Rev. Bill Laws and Dr. Sherm Franz in the early 1970s with breakfast at Bill Laws' house. In the '80s, it moved to FPC. "The emphasis of the men's group is support of one another. Life has all kinds of trauma, and in a confidential way, we listen and try to help. Nothing is recorded and nothing leaves the room," Bob Orben said. Members bring their breakfast to the 7:45 a.m. Friday sessions.

\*\*\*

The first homeless shelter in Columbus was established in 1986 at 606 California St. by the Bartholomew County Homeless Task Force. After three months, it closed due to inadequate facilities and support systems. The building had been occupied by homeless people 63 of those 90 days with a total of nine people staying there.[13] The following year, the Task Force relocated the shelter to 515 Seventh St., directly across from the church, where a parking lot now stands. Presbyterians were instrumental in this project, especially in the renovation of the property, though it was not a smooth move as several nearby residents protested. The Rev. David Liddle said First Presbyterian stood behind the task force's plans. "This is an opportunity for the community to show compassion and meet some genuine human needs," he said. The shelter, housed in a renovated, two-story building, began accepting people in June 1987.[14]

> "This (first homeless shelter in Columbus) is an opportunity for the community to show compassion and meet some genuine human needs."
>
> The Rev. David Liddle Jr.

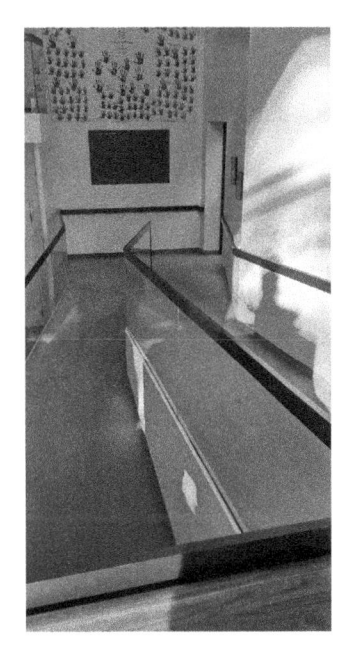

*A loggia with ramps for increased accessibility was put in during the 1981 building project. // Paul J. Hoffman*

\*\*\*

The church's largest building project since 1885 began in 1980 after a year of analysis, including interviews/surveys with hundreds of members. With nearly 250 children using the facilities each weekday, the congregation decided to build an educational wing north of the Donner Building. There was also a need for more bathrooms. By this time, the congregation had purchased the remaining homes in the block north of the church and owned the full half block between Seventh and Eighth streets between Franklin and the alley. So it had room to grow.

IDS Inc., an architectural firm from Champaign, Illinois, designed the building. In fact, IDS designed two buildings, giving the congregation a choice: a

---

13 Phil Johnston. "Shelter for homeless closes after 90 days." *The Republic*, Nov. 20, 1986.
14 "Homeless house warming Sunday." *The Republic*, June 12, 1987.

# 200 YEARS of FIRST PRESBYTERIAN CHURCH of COLUMBUS, INDIANA

## ISSUES

CLASSROOMS: Some almost cell-like...

Some so dark mold grows on the floors...

Electrical boxes within reach of curious fingers

...and never enough storage space.

By the late 1970s, issues with the church building necessitated a major renovation and expansion.

> "I agonized over that (decision on the 1981 building project) because we were committing our church to a big debt."
>
> Ben Bush

very modern structure like the Indiana Bell building across Franklin Street and one to reflect the architecture of the original structure. The congregational vote was almost 50/50, with the traditional design winning by the narrowest of margins. And yet, there was little animosity or lack of support for the design chosen.

Ben Bush credited local dentist Glenn Callaway with making an impassioned speech for the winning project on the night of the vote that Bush thinks might have convinced a few people to change their votes.

The $1.2 million addition consisted of 11,000 square feet. It housed day care children on weekdays and Sunday school classes on Sundays on the first floor. The second floor was designated a multipurpose room for youth activities.

## SOLUTIONS

In the New Wing — Classrooms

In the 1927 Addition — The Reeves Room

In the Original Building — The Laws Room

In the Donner Building — The Choir Room

The highlights of the 1981 building remodel and addition were highlighted in a brochure published by First Presbyterian. The $1.2 million, 11,000-square-foot addition consisted of space for day care children on weekdays and Sunday school classes on Sundays on the first floor, and a multipurpose room for youth activities on the second floor. Construction included a loggia to connect the three buildings with ramps to make most of the church handicap accessible, remodeling of the assembly room to remove the second floor and renaming it the Laws Room, remodeling of the 1927 addition to create more office space, and enclosing the stage in the gymnasium for a choir rehearsal room.

IDS's architects and interior designers were Irvin Schwartz and Harold Young.[15]

"I agonized over that (decision) because we were committing our church to a big debt," said Ben Bush.

The project included, along with the new wing, a loggia to connect the three buildings with ramps to make most of the church handicap accessible, remodeling of the assembly room to its original dimensions (removing the second floor) and renaming it the Laws Room, remodeling of the 1927 addition to create more office space, and enclosing the stage in the gymnasium for a choir rehearsal room. (The choir room houses a Steinway studio grand, the personal piano

---
15 "Presbyterians to mark completed renovation." *The Republic*, Sept. 10, 1981.

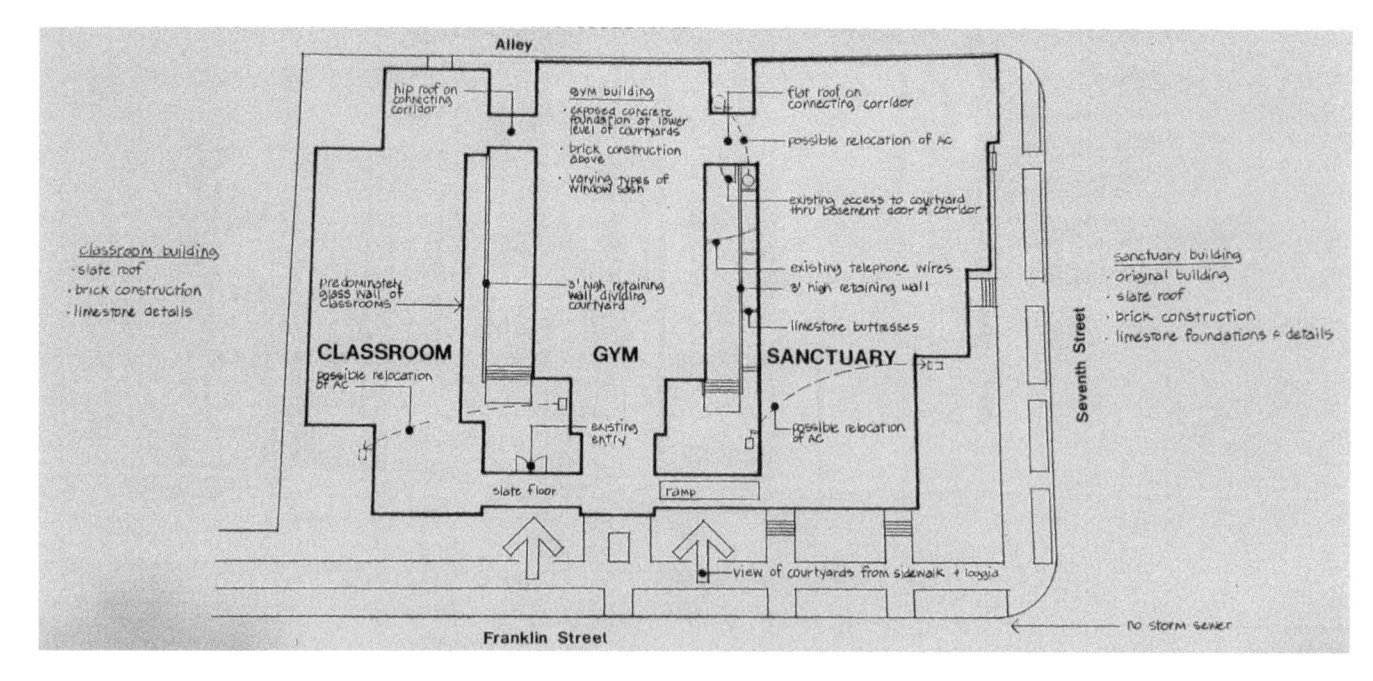

# 200 YEARS of FIRST PRESBYTERIAN CHURCH of COLUMBUS, INDIANA

An architectural drawing of the floor plan of the three buildings after the 1981 addition and renovation.

of longtime choir director Ida Edenburn Stark and was given to the church after her death.) On Sept. 27, 1981, the congregation dedicated the buildings and rededicated themselves to God's service. Accessibility was a big topic then, and in addition to making the campus easier to get around, the church also started offering large-print bulletins.

"I voted 'high tech' but have come to believe the congregation was right," wrote George Newlin. "'High tech' added to a 19th century building would have been a big gamble, whereas the building we built is most attractive."

On June 30, 1985, the congregation celebrated the 100th anniversary of the sanctuary (the 161st anniversary of First Presbyterian) and burned the mortgage for the new building that was taken out in 1981; this ended the congregation's longest period of debt in years. The mortgage burning ceremony took place in the Laws Room after regular services ended that day. During that service, 50-year members of the congregation were honored, and Ross Crump spoke on "Our Heritage."[16]

A columbarium was added in the courtyard between the sanctuary and the gymnasium in 1987. // Paul J. Hoffman

---

16 "First Presbyterian to burn mortgage for 161st birthday." *The Republic*, June 29, 1985.

The construction enhanced the "hospitality, access, ministry with young people and efficiency," according to Bailey. "We accomplished all this over a period of four years during challenging economic times."

\*\*\*

A columbarium, made possible by the vision and generous gift of Marion and Kay Dietrich, was constructed between the sanctuary and the Donner building in 1987. The columbarium, a departure from many Christian churches' tradition of burial in cemeteries, does however continue a tradition of burial in the church yard, with a peaceful, garden setting for in-urnment of cremated remains of church members and their families. "Our doctrine of resurrection is not affected by what happens to the physical body," the Rev. David Liddle Jr. said in 1989. "It (the columbarium) is a return to the old churchyard cemetery concept."[17] The first phase of construction provided masonry niches surrounded by plants, trees and stone walkways. Long-range plans included developing the north and south courtyards. The project was designed by Storrow Kinsella Partnership Inc. and built by Taylor Brothers Construction Co., both Columbus firms. The columbarium was the first of its kind in the Columbus area.[18]

A former men's restroom was transformed into a small chapel on the south side of the church in 1990. // Paul J. Hoffman

A small chapel, adjacent to the bell tower entrance to the church on Seventh Street, replaced a men's restroom in 1990. The rest-room had been added to the original building some time prior to this. The chapel was a gift of Herb and Barbara Hoover in memory of their son, Brian Hoover, an experienced mountain climber who died at the age of 26 while climbing Mount McKinley in Alaska in July 1987.[19] The chapel is a quiet space for small occasions of worship. Its stained-glass window, designed by Thelma Triplett and created by Diane Kitzinger, was given in memory of David Jones by family and friends. Jones, an active member of the congregation, trustee of the church, well-known interior designer and a syndicated newspaper columnist, died of a heart attack in November 1988 at the age of 59.[20] He had also been instrumental in the renovation that created the Laws Room out of the old assembly room. A variety of other donations helped build and furnish the chapel.[21]

\*\*\*

The double-digit inflation of the 1970s and '80s made the cost of housing soar in Columbus. Housing within the financial reach of many working families was practically nonexistent. The need for affordable housing sparked a First Presbyterian committee to gather 75 volunteers in October

---

17 Wheeler, Nancy. "More families choosing cremation." *The Republic*, Nov. 10, 1989.
18 "First Presbyterians build first columbarium memorial garden." *The Republic*, July 26, 1987.
19 Baumann, David. "Hope lingers for survival of mountaineer." *The Republic*, Aug. 3, 1987.
20 "Jones served community, common people." *The Republic*, Nov. 7, 1988.
21 Wheeler, Nancy. "Sacred space: Small chapel a gift of love." *The Republic*, Nov. 10, 1990.

## 200 YEARS of FIRST PRESBYTERIAN CHURCH of COLUMBUS, INDIANA

Photos from the 1982 member directory

200 YEARS of FIRST PRESBYTERIAN CHURCH of COLUMBUS, INDIANA

Photos from the 1982 member directory

Housing Partnerships Inc. arose from a home restoration program First Presbyterian started in 1990. It now operates as Thrive Alliance.

and November 1989 to repair the home of an elderly widow on Pearl Street. Veera Wagoner, 72, was on a fixed income and couldn't afford to make necessary repairs to her 146-year-old home. The house was selected after a suggestion from a worker at Sans Souci, where Wagoner volunteered until back problems forced her to stop. The church allocated $8,200 for materials and a salary for a consultant.[22]

Fixing that home was just the first item on the task force's checklist. The long-range plan was to work with other churches to form a nonprofit to help assist with Columbus' housing issues.

The group achieved those goals, forming Housing Partnerships Inc. in 1990 with seven other churches. HPI's purpose was to buy structurally sound but run-down houses, repair and refurbish them, and sell them to qualified low-income families through special mortgage arrangements with local banks. "In a way the program is an anti-poverty program since one of the fastest ways to get out of poverty is to have stable housing, except this is just part of the overall process," HPI director Bob Hyatt told a reporter.[23]

HPI was backed by Irwin-Sweeney-Miller Foundation, the Heritage Fund and contributions. By July 1990, HPI had 150 volunteers working on three houses.[24] In early 1999, Housing Partnerships completed its 100th project. It now does business as Thrive Alliance and has developed more than 550 affordable homes throughout the region.[25]

One of the major projects the group tackled early on was transforming the iconic red brick National Guard Armory building at the southwest corner of Seventh and Franklin streets into 25 apartments for seniors. The idea was floated by Darrell Unsworth, an HPI staffer, in 1992, when the building became vacant. Construction began in spring 1995, and the $2 million project was dedicated in January 1997. The apartments ranged from 600-square-foot, one-bedroom apartments, including four handicapped-accessible units, to efficiency units.[26] The church still maintains a relationship with the Armory Apartments and conducts monthly birthday parties there.

> "One of the fastest ways to get out of poverty is to have stable housing."
>
> Bob Hyatt

\*\*\*

Another building project was undertaken thousands of miles away. Several youth work groups and medical missions from the Columbus area, includ-

---

22  MacNair, Andrea. "For her, home's where the help is." *The Republic*, Oct. 30, 1989.
23  Harmon, John. "Building boom: Volunteer group hammers away to meet demand for affordable local housing." *The Republic*, July 15, 1990.
24  Ibid.
25  Thrive Alliance. https://thrive-alliance.org/housing/
26  Blair, Brian. "Seniors look forward to Armory dedication, moving in." *The Republic*. Jan. 25, 1997.

Volunteers work in Calnali, Mexico, hometown of First Presbyterian member Juana Watson. First Presbyterian and Fairlawn sent members to help with a building mission in 1993. Other groups joined in through the years.

First Presbyterian has provided hot meals to anyone who needs one on Friday nights for the past 30 years. This photo is from 1996.

ing many Presbyterians, had visited Calnali, Mexico, hometown of First Presbyterian member Juana Watson. The first such group to travel to the "poor village" went in July 1993 and consisted of 27 people from Fairlawn and First Presbyterian churches. Much of the village was without electricity and running water. Friends of Calnali, a group spearheaded by Presbyterians, undertook a major rebuilding project on an existing structure in Calnali to provide not only living accommodations, including indoor plumbing, but also a place where the medical teams could do their work and a place for social activities. The building also served as a community center. The Columbus group also provided local children with a summer camp experience, which by the end of the week attracted more than 300 children. The "Americanos" also distributed clothing, toys and school supplies. Grateful families presented gifts of bananas and chili peppers. On Sunday, the visitors attended Catholic Mass with the villagers in a simple church with wooden benches and kneelers.[27]

What the Presbyterians started in Calnali, others joined and built upon. Watson and Gene Foldenauer, chairman of the foreign language department at Columbus North High School, led annual trips to Calnali for several years. High school students spent their spring breaks helping do whatever was needed, whether that was pouring concrete or playing with the local children. While in Mexico, students stayed in a building purchased by First Presbyterian.

Watson founded Su Casa in Columbus, which brought awareness about Latino/Hispanic issues and race relations in the community. She also either founded or co-founded Badges without Borders, Indiana Multi-Ethnic Conference and Indiana Women's Diversity Network.

\*\*\*

New ministries continued to be added to the long list of outreach programs through which the congregation has sought to help its neighbors. The singles ministry, Single-Minded Ministry, was a successful program reaching far beyond one congregation in the late 1990s.

The Stephen Ministry quietly offers the help of trained volunteers to the grieving, the lonely, the

---

27 Eynon, Laurie. "Friends in a strange land: Mexico trip emphasizes similarity of people." *The Republic*, July 31, 1993.

disaffected; anyone in need of comfort or assistance could come for help on a one-to-one basis.

Longtime member Janet Sharpe was the chairwoman of the first Columbus CROP Walk, which attracted 183 people and two dogs for a 10-kilometer jaunt on a rainy October day in 1985 that raised nearly $5,000. Twenty-five percent of the proceeds went to hot meal sites in the city.[28] CROP (Christian Rural Overseas Program) walks aim to "end hunger one step at a time."

In 1993, we started a hot meals program, one of several sponsored by local churches offering food and fellowship for anyone in the community. It continues to this day, with meals served each Friday evening. Average attendance varies from 30 to 80. All food is donated by the volunteers who serve the meals and the churches and community sites that host them. Sarah Sanders headed up this effort for the past 20 years.

THE WORSHIP ALTERNATIVE is alive and well and meeting on Sunday Mornings at 11:30 a.m.

On Easter Sunday 1999, the church began a new outreach program, an alternative worship service. Organized to explore the need for a second service because of increasing attendance, a worship task force quickly came to realize that the church needed not only a second service but a different service to fill needs not being met within the congregation and within the community. After more than six months' study, the task force proposed and the Session approved the new service, which recognized that just as all Christians are not at the same place on the faith pilgrimage, all Christians do not find expression for the worship of God in the same way. While rooted in Presbyterian theology and tradition, the alternative service was shorter, more diverse, and with more lay participation than the traditional service. This alternative service lasted a few years, but the church has been open to trying various types of services since.

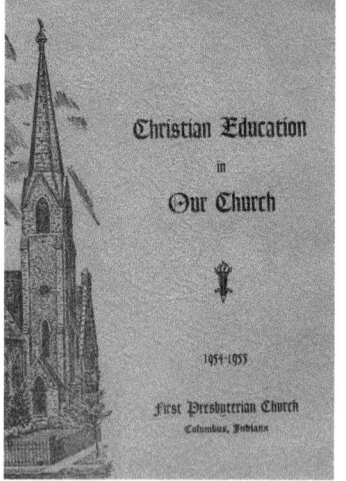

Sarah Hunt was named Woman of Faith for 1996 by the Women's Ministries Program Area at the 208th General Assembly of the Presbyterian Church (USA).

\*\*\*\*

At the 208th General Assembly of the Presbyterian Church (USA), Sarah Hunt was named Woman of Faith for 1996 by the Women's Ministries Program Area. The theme for the award was "Sharing Wisdom," and Hunt was honored "as a distinguished peace activist, enlightened civic educator and a mentor to generations." It was her 50th year of membership at First Presbyterian, where she served as director of Christian education from 1950 to 1956.

A longtime community activist, Hunt was also a recipient of The Republic's Woman of the Year award in 1989 and the National Jefferson Award in 1982. A member of First Presbyterian from 1946 to her death in 1998, she was a charter member of Columbus Peace Fellowship in 1967 and was a member of the Columbus NAACP.[29]

---

28 "CROP Walk raises nearly $5,000 despite pouring rain." *The Republic*, Oct. 23, 1985.
29 "Community activist, volunteer Hunt dies." *The Republic,* Jan. 16, 1998.

"She was a saint for sure," said longtime member Ann Jones, who viewed Hunt as a mentor and surrogate mother. "But she had some seediness to that sainthood."

In the 1990s, Hunt also led an Earth Spirit group, an ecumenical effort that "pushed the boundaries," as the Rev. Janet Lowery said, with practices like "meditation, embodiment, lots of things that men hadn't been exposed to. Not that they were against it; they just hadn't been exposed to it."

Hunt was not the first Columbus Presbyterian woman to be honored by the national church. In 1960, Jessie Cummins was made an honorary member of the National Board of Missions for her Bible study developed for migrant workers of Arizona, called "Dear Colossians – Dear Arizonans – Says Paul." While wintering in Arizona, Cummins devoted much time and energy trying to better the living conditions of migrant workers and Native Americans in the area.

Jessie Cummins was made an honorary member of the National Board of Missions for her Bible study developed for migrant workers of Arizona.

\*\*\*

By 1995, the Reuter organ was in such dire need of major repair that it was decided to replace it and to completely renovate and redecorate the sanctuary at the same time. This large and expensive project was fully subscribed on the first day. The new Casavant Frères, a 47-rank organ, was dedicated Sept. 17, 1995.

The American Organist magazine featured our new Casavant Frères organ as its cover story six months after the instrument was placed in the sanctuary in 1995.

The organ, which took several months to custom build, tune and adjust, cost $450,000.[30] Including the renovation needed to install it, the price tag went over $850,000. The decision to sell the old organ to Asbury United Methodist in the city for roughly $30,000 and purchase the new organ wasn't unanimously popular with the congregation, according to then director of music Ray Hass. Though some considered the purchase a bargain.

---

30  Blair, Brian. "Tuning in to new sound: First Presbyterian dedicating $450,000 organ in special services." *The Republic,* Sept. 16, 1995.

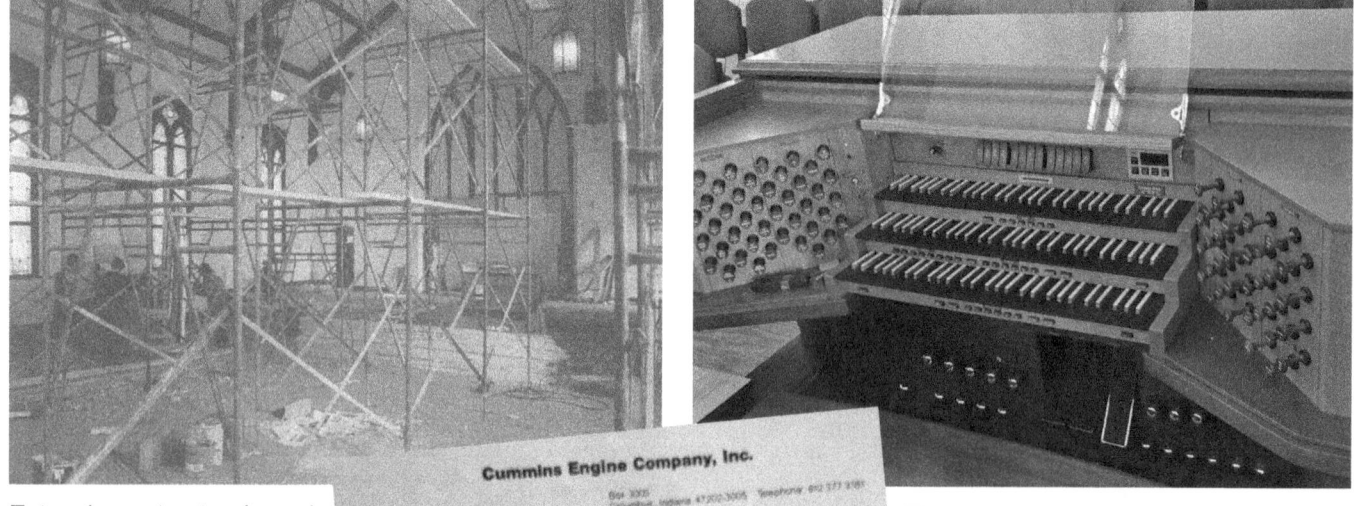

# 200 YEARS of FIRST PRESBYTERIAN CHURCH of COLUMBUS, INDIANA

Extensive structural and cosmetic repairs of the sanctuary were necessary to accommodate the new organ.

"Today, it would have cost $2 million," Zack Ellison said.

"The preliminary work (in getting the organ) was done by Ron McMillin," Hass recalled. "He was the general chair of that committee. We wouldn't have gotten that instrument if not for him. If people weren't happy with it or had questions, he would go talk to them at their homes and discuss it."

Since the new organ needed to be tuned for its space, it was decided to remodel the sanctuary. That required the carpeting and pews be removed. And the ceiling, which had been canvas, got a double thickness of drywall.

The new organ became a selling point for First Presbyterian. People wanted to see and hear the instrument, whose pipes reached as high as 40 feet, encased in walnut at the front of the sanctuary. A recital series started just a week after the dedication, and several concerts, many featuring the organ, followed for several years. There were concerts with a classical guitarist, string quartet and brass quartet, and Ray Hass and Cindy McMillin (flute) performed duets.

Marion Dietrich, a Cummins executive, was also instrumental in leading the charge for the new organ. "He funded the maintenance fund," Bob Hyatt said. "That was such a powerful thing for me."

Ed Bruenjes, the organist at Asbury, had the ability to disassemble, fix and reassemble the old organ, which was why that congregation purchased it. It's still in use there.

The console is the control center for the organ. Walnut, oak, rosewood, maple and cherry were used in building the console. Left: A letter from Jim Henderson to Marion Dietrich informing him of Henderson's pledge to donate $50,000 toward the organ project.

\*\*\*

In 1983, the rift between the northern and southern branches of the Presbyterian Church, a result of the causes and effects of the Civil War, was at last healed, and the two churches became one again, to be known as the Presbyterian Church (USA). An earlier merger, in 1959, of two branches of the northern church had given the denomination the name of United Presbyterian Church in the United States of America, and for 24 years we were the First United Presbyterian Church of Columbus.

\*\*\*

David M. Liddle Jr. was formally installed as pastor on Aug. 29, 1982, after spending five years as associate pastor here. The congregation couldn't immediately name him pastor after Bailey left, and it was an odd time in the interim.

"There was a requirement that you bring in an interim for 18 months or so in-between pastors," Zack Ellison said. "It's supposed to be a process to get over the last guy or woman and to move on to the new person."

"We struggled with how to do a search when one of the candidates was already here," said Sherry Stark, who was on the pastor selection committee. "Our first decision to make was, 'Do we want to call David?' We did all the steps necessary to make that decision, and we decided yes. Some thought we should do a big search, but we thought that was kind of unnecessary

David Liddle Jr.

and in some ways unkind to David."

Prior to coming here, Liddle had been assistant, then associate pastor at First Presbyterian in Downey, California. A native of Des Moines, Iowa, he graduated from Northwestern University with an English degree. He received a master's in religion and church history from the University of Iowa and his Master of Divinity, cum laude, from Pittsburgh Theological Seminary.[31]

According to Liddle, during his first interview here, the pastor search committee asked if it would be all right to take a break so they could all watch the then-popular TV series, "Roots." He was fine with that.

While in Columbus, Liddle was part of the originating committee to get Hospice of South Central Indiana, formerly Bartholomew County Area Hospice, started and was instrumental in helping Housing Partnerships Inc. get off the ground. Like many of our ministers before him, Liddle served on many boards in the community.[32]

"The startup was rocky; I'd neglected to do my grief work upon leaving my first call, so it was a struggle to find my footing," Liddle said "Were it not for the warm welcome I and my family received from new colleagues, staff and church members, many of whom became dear friends, I might have languished in a haze of regret. But I remained confident that God

---

31 "Liddle assumes Presbyterian pastorate." *The Republic*, June 30, 1982.
32 Wheeler, Nancy. "Liddle follows call to new challenges." *The Republic*, Aug. 2, 1997.

# 200 YEARS of FIRST PRESBYTERIAN CHURCH of COLUMBUS, INDIANA

## 50+-Year Members - 1994

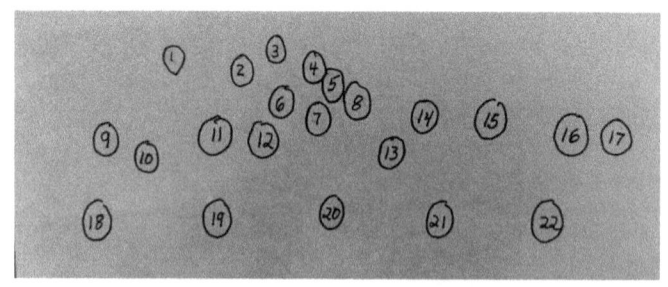

1. John Cummings
2. James Jewell
3. Jiggs Thompson
4. George Doup
5. Cal Wright
6. John Rowell
7. Bob Thompson
8. Cal Brand
9. Peggy Stevenson
10. Mary Jones Hamilton
11. Ruth Halvorsen
12. Lenore Fitzgibbon
13. Betty Brand
14. Helen Rowell
15. Charles Hathaway
16. Roseada Walters
17. Fern McClung
18. Jerald Dunlap
19. Maxine Dunlap
20. Mary Jane Butler
21. Mary Bottoroff
22. Alta Redmond

# 200 YEARS of FIRST PRESBYTERIAN CHURCH of COLUMBUS, INDIANA

## 50+-Year Members - 1999

From left, front row: Beryl Hathaway, Mary Hamilton, Helen Rowell, Betty Brand, Cal Brand, Jane Phillips, Warren Phillips; second row: George Doup, Alta Redmond, Mary Jane Butler, Roberta Thompson, Bill Thompson, Imogene Welch, Bob Welch, Pauline Crump, Lenore Fitzgibbon, Ruth Halvorsen; third row: John Cummins, Cal Wright, Bill Davis, Jiggs Thompson, Marge Silva, Fern McClung, Peggy Stevenson.

Pat and Ben Bush

Sherm Franz

Zack Ellison

David and Susie Jones

Mary and Bob Orben with David Bailey.

Mary Ann McCray

Waldo Harrison

Vern Jorck

Ann Jones

had called me to First Church, so I persevered, and the rest (as they say) is history."

He was described as a handsome, gentle man who loved to ride motorcycles and loved his family.

In 1997, after 20 years on the staff and 15 as pastor, Liddle resigned to accept a pastorate at St. Andrew Presbyterian Church in Indianapolis. His ministry was the fourth longest in our congregation's history. He and his wife, Lorene, had been important parts of the community, as well. Lorene Liddle served as an elder, the first minister's wife to be elected to that office.

"They take their Christian faith seriously in terms of serving others," he said of First Presbyterian upon leaving. "They have never failed to step up to the challenges and issues that needed to be addressed."[33]

From left: The congregation's first female minister was Frances Unsell, who served as associate from December 1983 to early 1987. When Unsell left, Janet Lowery came on board as interim associate minister. Lowery became lead pastor when David Liddle left in 1997 and shortly thereafter, Norie Erickson was hired as head of staff, marking the first time in FPC history that two women led the pastoral team.

> "They take their Christian faith seriously in terms of serving others."
>
> David Liddle

\*\*\*

Shortly after the congregation chose Liddle as pastor, it also called its first woman minister, Frances Unsell, as associate. Unsell served in that capacity from December 1983 until she accepted a call in early 1987 from the Program Agency of the Presbyterian Church (USA) in New York City to serve as associate for women's programs, Eastern Area Office, Presbyterian Women. A native of Pine Bluff, Arkansas, Unsell was responsible for staffing First Presbyterian's adult and children's education programs, the library, newcomer orientation, fellowship activities, and the Calling and Caring Ministry, in addition to doing pastoral calling and occasional preaching.[34]

When Unsell left, Janet Lowery came as interim associate minister. Originally from Indianapolis, Lowery was an assistant pastor at Greenwood Presbyterian Church and was coordinator of the Big Sisters program in Johnson County before coming to Columbus.[35] Because she was coming as an interim, it didn't have to be put before the congregation for a vote, Lowery said. "I called and asked if they wanted an interim," she said. "He (Liddle) said, 'We'll give it a try.'"

The move worked out well as Lowery stayed until 1999, becoming lead pastor after Liddle left in 1997. She was the first pastor here who had been divorced.

Of her time with Liddle and Hass, Lowery said the three worked well together despite having different strengths.

---

33  Ibid.
34  "Frances Unsell leaving First Presbyterian." *The Republic*, Feb. 21, 1987.
35  "Assistant pastor installed." (Johnson County) *Daily Journal*, Nov. 23, 1985.

200 YEARS of FIRST PRESBYTERIAN CHURCH of COLUMBUS, INDIANA

Left: Photos from an all-church picnic in 1987. Above: a child prays during a skit. Below: A senior high Sunday school session in the mid-1990s.

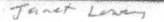

103

# 200 YEARS of FIRST PRESBYTERIAN CHURCH of COLUMBUS, INDIANA

The group found that out from an outside source when they went to a workshop once. As part of the workshop, all participants took the Myers-Briggs personality test to see what types of personalities they had. When the results came in, "they said, 'We have never seen a pastoral staff as diverse as you three are, and your congregation is very lucky because everyone has someone to go to,'" Lowery recalled.

Liddle concentrated on worship, the building, elders and finance. Hass worked with the music and deacons. Lowery worked with nurturing, Christian education, men's and women's groups, and fun things, she said.

When Liddle left, Norie Erickson came on board as interim head of staff in December 1998 and stayed until June 1999, marking the first time FPC was led by two women, not a common occurrence in those days.

"We made a good team," Erickson said of that era. "People responded well to my preaching, and we began to fill up the pews on a regular basis."

Lowery agreed. "We worked together well; they (congregation) loved it."

"We received great benefit from having some great women ministers," Stark said. "Norie with her candor and openness, Janet was great fun, and Frances was a character."

Much of Lowery's passion concerned feminism and inclusive language. Roe v. Wade was a big topic at General Assembly when Lowery was at First Presbyterian. She said she would go to General Assembly and give testimony on why Christians should be supportive of a woman's right to choose. It wasn't always well received. However, the General Assembly eventually made statements on economic justice at the Mexico/USA border and on abortion (siding with a woman's right to choose). "The General Assembly was saying these things not because we're a bunch of liberals, but because it's in scripture," she said.

At the time, there was only one service, but due to popular demand, a second service was added in the gym after the first service, starting on Easter Sunday 1999, Erickson said.

"My time at FPC was the highlight of my career," she said.

In May 1999, Lowery, after 11 years as associate pastor, resigned to become pastor of North Springfield Presbyterian Church in Akron, Ohio. Erickson, originally from Pennsylvania, had been an English teacher at Columbus High School and chaplain at Four Seasons, an assisted-living care facility in Columbus.

\*\*\*

In 1987, the congregation welcomed a pastor from Denmark for six weeks. The Rev. Knud Ochsner preached, taught and met with church and community groups while here. Ochsner came to Columbus as part of a program that brought pastors from different parts of the world to the United States to share in the life work of the congregations.[36]

\*\*\*

The Rev. Knud Ochsner, left, chats with David Liddle. Ochsner, a visiting pastor from Denmark, spent six weeks here in 1987.

---

36 "First Presbyterian Church welcomes Danish pastor." *The Republic*, Sept. 26, 1987.

# 200 YEARS of FIRST PRESBYTERIAN CHURCH of COLUMBUS, INDIANA

The congregation celebrated the 200th anniversary of the Presbyterian Church (USA) on May 7, 1989, with a 1789 worship service, styled after the type that might have been typical in Colonial America. According to Puritan customs of the time, that meant men and boys all were to sit on the south side of the church and the women and girls on the north side. Members were invited to wear dark clothing. Meanwhile, everyone was expected to refrain from reading anything, except what the minister has been reading or citing; and abstaining from all whispering, salutations, sleeping, smiling, gazing about and "all other indecent behavior." Janet Lowery preached the sermon on "God Chose Our Heritage." Ted Sharpe, Judy Labold, and Clyde Saums arranged the service.

\*\*\*

VIMCare, formerly Volunteers in Medicine, opened on Sept. 26, 1996, as our community's solution to a critical lack of access to primary health care for low-income, uninsured Bartholomew County residents. Dr. Sherman Franz, a First Presbyterian member, was involved in launching the effort in the old license branch at 836 Jackson St. The free service was supported by many organizations, starting with a two-year funding commitment by Rotary Club of Columbus. More than 100 medical professionals and 100 community volunteers donated their time, and more than 300 residents were served in the first month of operation.[37] The program is now under the Columbus Regional Health umbrella and operates out of Nexus Park.

\*\*\*

A group from the church led an effort to honor veterans in the mid-1990s that ended with the erection of the Veterans Memorial on the courthouse lawn. Some Vietnam veterans who belonged to the church sought to get a memorial built, according to Zack Ellison, who was on the committee. The group met at Veterans of Foreign Wars and American Legion posts in

Church members led the effort that resulted in the Bartholomew County Veterans Memorial. // Bartholomew County Historical Society

town to discuss ideas. At first, the group targeted the Second Street Bridge. Bob Hayes, a state representative, agreed to push a resolution to rename the bridge Veterans Memorial Bridge. But the group met with Larry Kleinhenz, then a new county commissioner and chairman of the memorial committee, and he said, "Let's do something bigger," Ellison said.

Will Miller, son of J. Irwin Miller and former chairman of Irwin Management Co., and Harry McCawley, associate editor of *The Republic*, got on board with the project, which was funded through a lot of donations. Dunlap Construction donated labor at cost. Sylvia Kiel obtained a cement donation. "We did it for $870,000," Ellison said. "Without their help, it would have cost $1.6 million or more."

The memorial, consisting of 25 40-foot-tall, tightly packed limestone pillars with inscriptions of letters

---

37 Maschino, Brenda. "Rotary fills clinic's monthly prescription." *The Republic*, Nov. 5, 1996.

home from veterans, was dedicated on May 30, 1997. The project also included walkways (Veterans Walk of Honor) on the courthouse square with dedications to veterans inscribed in bricks (nearly 4,000 were purchased by the deadline). The dedication of the memorial coincided with the revival of a Memorial Day celebration on the courthouse lawn. [38]

\*\*\*

During the 1980s there was concern for the "graying of the congregation." Membership from 1970 to 1980 was static, and few young people joined. A children's sermon often drew no more than five children. Beginning in the mid-1990s this trend began to reverse.

Lowery recalls a time when there were virtually no children in the sanctuary. Barb and Rich Newton's children were about it. The Newtons started inviting friends who had children to come to church, and before long the sanctuary was once again filled with young ones. "It's so cyclical, (but) it just goes to show you that one member or family can make a difference," Lowery said.

Membership in 1990 was 559 active members. (This number reflects a change in how the congregation was counted as well as a loss in membership.)

\*\*\*

The church went all out for its 175th anniversary, celebrating with a whole slew of events spanning several months.

Carol Berkey wrote a book on the history of First Presbyterian Church for the 175th anniversary in 1999.

On particular Sundays starting on Dec. 27, 1998, members dressed as prominent historical figures to help tell the congregation's story during a Moment for History segment during worship.

A Heritage Communion Service was conducted on Feb. 7, 1999, where several members dressed in 1800s attire to help set the tone. The program for the service noted, "We cannot recreate the past, but we honor those who have come before us as they worshipped the same God and our Savior Jesus Christ."

The congregation also provided a display of heirloom quilts, planted a tree on the courthouse lawn and conducted a choral festival with the First United Methodist and North Christian adult choirs.

Ray Hass, the minister of music, wrote a hymn to commemorate the celebration; it was introduced at services on June 6. His words in part:

*O God of past and future of this church,*

*We lay before you our rich heritage,*

*Remembering all the lives of those before us,*

*Who sacrificed much so that we might live.*[39]

The June 27 service included a children's sermon given by Rick and Mary Martin that discussed the new, quilted banner, put together by Mary Martin, Natalie Roll, Francey Cooper, Virginia Kinnaman and Janet Ward, for the anniversary. The children's

---

[38] McCawley, Harry. "Dedication today: City gathers to salute veterans' memories," *The Republic*. May 30, 1997.
[39] Blair, Brian. "Church celebrates 175 years of spiritual strength." *The Republic*. June 26, 1999.

# 200 YEARS of FIRST PRESBYTERIAN CHURCH of COLUMBUS, INDIANA

Members plant a tree on the courthouse square on April 24, 1999, in honor of the church's 175th anniversary.

Above: Women work on a quilted banner made in honor of the 175th anniversary. Below: Merry Carmichael explains that the church goes on, even when people change, during children's time. Each child received a church history timeline prepared by Merry's husband, Tom.

sermon talked about how the church was much like a quilt, in that "each person is a part of that quilt ... important to the whole design, but they come from many different places. All the bits and pieces work together to make a quilt just as all the different people work together to make a church."

Fifty-year members were honored at the service; this included Calvin (Cal) Wright, who had joined First Presbyterian in 1922. He passed away at the age of 90 in 2002, just after celebrating his 80th year as a member of the congregation.

After services on that day, the church conducted a birthday celebration at noon at Donner Park, including a pitch-in dinner, along with games and songs from the 1800s.

# 200 YEARS of FIRST PRESBYTERIAN CHURCH of COLUMBUS, INDIANA

Building plans from 1995

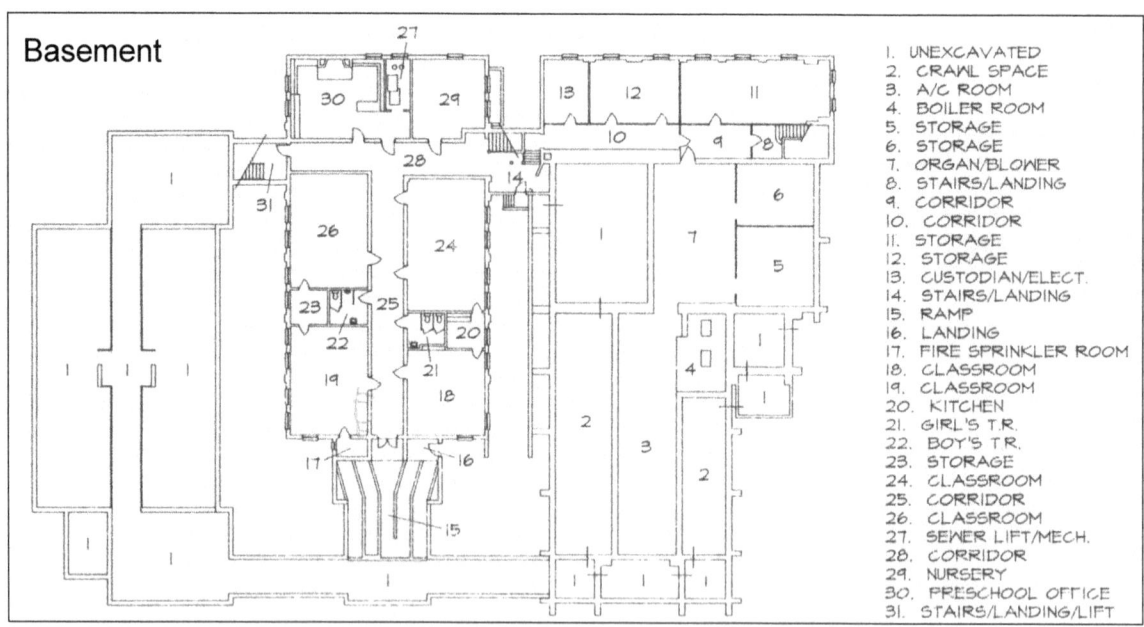

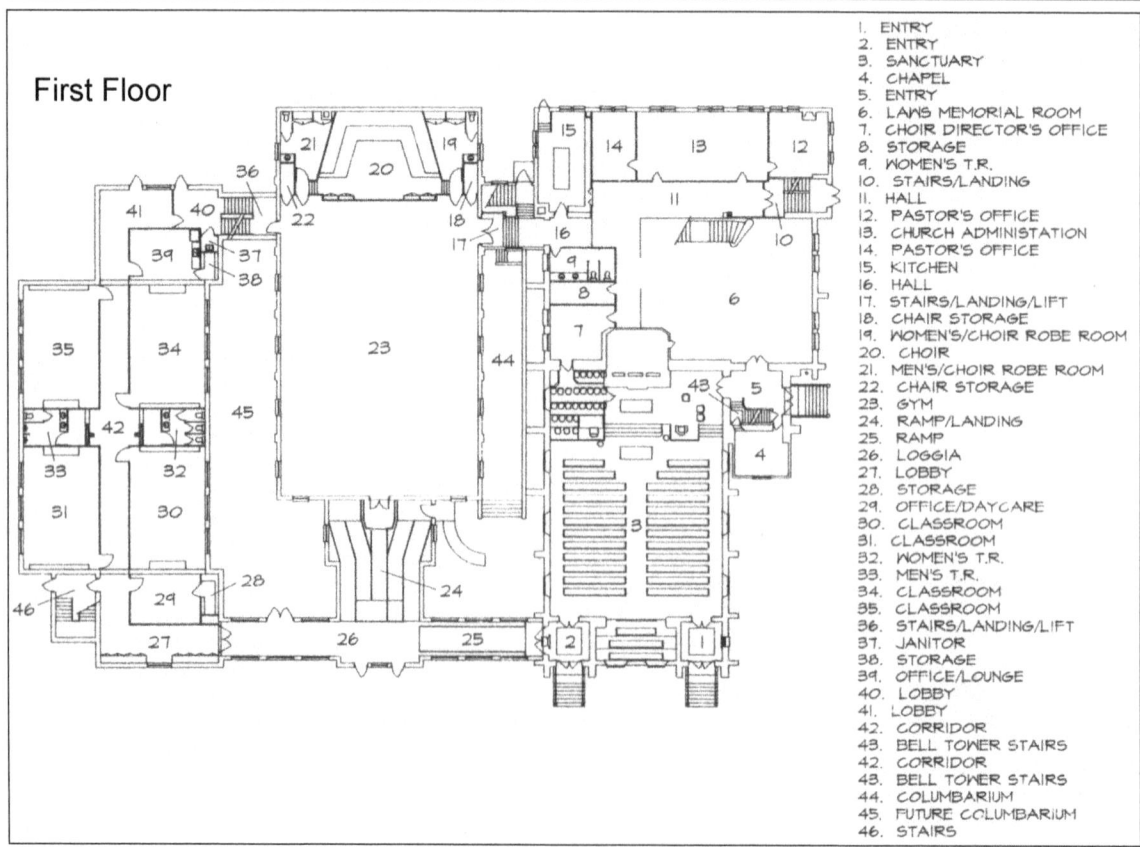

## Basement

1. UNEXCAVATED
2. CRAWL SPACE
3. A/C ROOM
4. BOILER ROOM
5. STORAGE
6. STORAGE
7. ORGAN/BLOWER
8. STAIRS/LANDING
9. CORRIDOR
10. CORRIDOR
11. STORAGE
12. STORAGE
13. CUSTODIAN/ELECT.
14. STAIRS/LANDING
15. RAMP
16. LANDING
17. FIRE SPRINKLER ROOM
18. CLASSROOM
19. CLASSROOM
20. KITCHEN
21. GIRL'S T.R.
22. BOY'S T.R.
23. STORAGE
24. CLASSROOM
25. CORRIDOR
26. CLASSROOM
27. SEWER LIFT/MECH.
28. CORRIDOR
29. NURSERY
30. PRESCHOOL OFFICE
31. STAIRS/LANDING/LIFT

## First Floor

1. ENTRY
2. ENTRY
3. SANCTUARY
4. CHAPEL
5. ENTRY
6. LAWS MEMORIAL ROOM
7. CHOIR DIRECTOR'S OFFICE
8. STORAGE
9. WOMEN'S T.R.
10. STAIRS/LANDING
11. HALL
12. PASTOR'S OFFICE
13. CHURCH ADMINISTATION
14. PASTOR'S OFFICE
15. KITCHEN
16. HALL
17. STAIRS/LANDING/LIFT
18. CHAIR STORAGE
19. WOMEN'S/CHOIR ROBE ROOM
20. CHOIR
21. MEN'S/CHOIR ROBE ROOM
22. CHAIR STORAGE
23. GYM
24. RAMP/LANDING
25. RAMP
26. LOGGIA
27. LOBBY
28. STORAGE
29. OFFICE/DAYCARE
30. CLASSROOM
31. CLASSROOM
32. WOMEN'S T.R.
33. MEN'S T.R.
34. CLASSROOM
35. CLASSROOM
36. STAIRS/LANDING/LIFT
37. JANITOR
38. STORAGE
39. OFFICE/LOUNGE
40. LOBBY
41. LOBBY
42. CORRIDOR
43. BELL TOWER STAIRS
42. CORRIDOR
43. BELL TOWER STAIRS
44. COLUMBARIUM
45. FUTURE COLUMBARIUM
46. STAIRS

## Second Floor

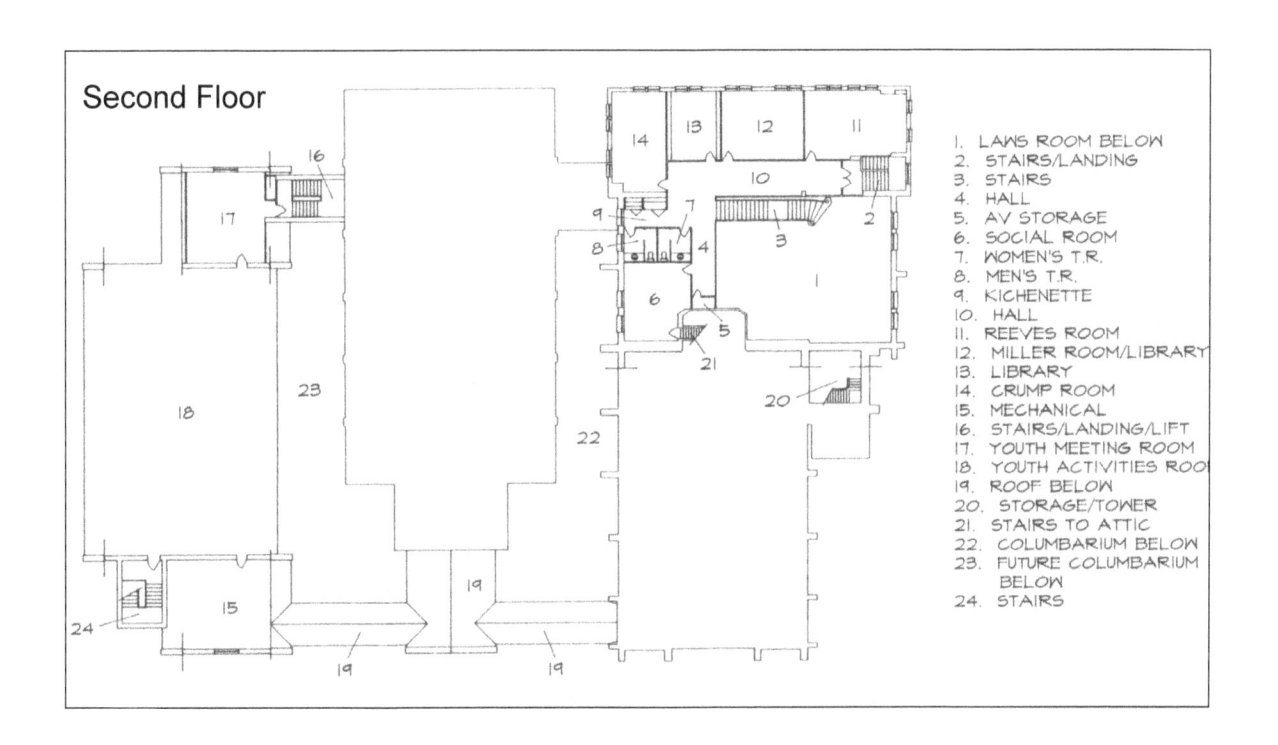

1. LAWS ROOM BELOW
2. STAIRS/LANDING
3. STAIRS
4. HALL
5. AV STORAGE
6. SOCIAL ROOM
7. WOMEN'S T.R.
8. MEN'S T.R.
9. KICHENETTE
10. HALL
11. REEVES ROOM
12. MILLER ROOM/LIBRARY
13. LIBRARY
14. CRUMP ROOM
15. MECHANICAL
16. STAIRS/LANDING/LIFT
17. YOUTH MEETING ROOM
18. YOUTH ACTIVITIES ROOM
19. ROOF BELOW
20. STORAGE/TOWER
21. STAIRS TO ATTIC
22. COLUMBARIUM BELOW
23. FUTURE COLUMBARIUM BELOW
24. STAIRS

Congregation photo, 1999

# The 21st Century

**First Presbyterian** entered a new century with a new pastor. The Rev. Richard "Dick" Underdahl-Peirce started preaching here in May 1999 and was officially installed as the church's 16th pastor on Aug. 29. He came to Columbus from Junction City, Kansas, with a rich and varied background and a wealth of experience. The son of Presbyterian missionaries, he received his elementary education in what was then called The Cameroons, West Africa, and went to high school in Long Island, New York. He was a graduate of Princeton Theological Seminary.

Underdahl-Peirce had been closely associated with mission causes in his former pastorates, including emergency shelters, care for the elderly and youth-related activities. He was said to have had a good sense of humor, had good ideas and showed a great deal of passion.

One of the things that the congregation introduced during his time here was the Mission Support Committee in 2005. As its name implies, this group provides funding for various missions the church supports. It's supported by the foundation, which allots one-third of its budget every year to Mission Support. In 2023, Mission Support gave $45,000 total to a variety of worthwhile causes.

Dick and Ruth Underdahl-Peirce and their children, Jon and Beth Ann, moved to Columbus in June 1999. They stayed until 2005, moving to Minnesota thereafter.

\*\*\*

One of the church's newest ministries during this time was Su Casa, a local Hispanic resource center. Translated "your house," it opened May 6, 1999, at 1871 State St., in response to the growing Hispanic population here. The initial goal was educating newcomers in English, American laws and parenting skills. First Presbyterian member Juana Watson was the first director. Roughly 35 people from various churches helped get the project started, with First Presbyterian covering much of the initial expenses and supplying many of the committee members.[1]

Richard Underdahl-Peirce

---

1 Showalter, Doug. "Community center recognizes Hispanic population." *The Republic*, April 28, 1999.

Its mission "is to increase self-sufficiency, health, economic independence, education and ensure Latino families feel safe and belong here. Su Casa believes that all residents should have equitable access to the tools and support needed to be successful regardless of socio-economic or immigration status, gender identity, sexual orientation, race or beliefs."[2]

Su Casa has since opened a Seymour office and expanded its services. Current First Presbyterian pastor Felipe Martinez and congregation member Amy Hale sit on its board of directors.

\*\*\*

Ruth Billington was associate pastor from 2001-05. With Underdahl-Peirce's departure, the congregation brought in Nancy Howard as interim pastor in late 2005. She served Presbyterian congregations in Indianapolis and Bluffton before coming here and was called as pastor of Christ Presbyterian in McCordsville when she left.

\*\*\*

The next pastor called was the Rev. Dr. Robert (Rob) Hugh Craig, who arrived in October 2007 after serving churches in St. Louis; Albuquerque, New Mexico; and Washington, D.C. He had also been executive director at Ghost Ranch, an education and retreat Center in Abiquiu, New Mexico.

He came here partially at the recommendation of Cal Brand, whose family befriended the Craigs several years earlier when they were in St. Louis. When there was a vacancy in the pulpit here, Brand and his wife met the Craigs in New Mexico for a visit.

"He wanted to get back in the parish to finish out before retirement," Brand said. "At the same time, we had a pastor nominating committee, and some of us were feeling some discouragement. I suggested to Rob that he contact our committee. And lo and behold, he got in touch with them. That was such a treat. He was a good pastor. It was providence."

Craig's impact on Columbus was felt both within and outside the walls of the building. He signed all correspondence with "Peace and Justice." It didn't take folks long to discover that he lived by those words. Craig participated in activities such as Healthy Communities and founded Different Ministers.

He was an avid golfer, and he and his wife, Sharon, were well liked by the membership. He enjoyed spending time in the community and "was a good preacher, a meticulous administrator," said Mary Ann McCray.

He had a favorite Psalm verse that he would act out with hand gestures and funny sounds when leading the children's time at church services, and his daily prayer was, "Thank you for the gift of this day not promised."

*Robert (Rob) Hugh Craig*

---

2 Su Casa website, https://sucasaindiana.org/mission-and-history/

# 200 YEARS of FIRST PRESBYTERIAN CHURCH of COLUMBUS, INDIANA

> "As much as any minister/wife combination, they (Rob and Sharon Craig) brought so much to the church. Rob Craig brought a warmth and gentle humor to his time as pastor at First Presbyterian Church."
>
> Sherry Stark

"He was a favorite of mine," Sherry Stark said. "As much as any minister/wife combination, they brought so much to the church. Rob Craig brought a warmth and gentle humor to his time as pastor at First Presbyterian Church. He was often spotted around town driving his aging turquoise truck and wearing his cowboy hat."

The Craigs entertained the Session at their home every year, with Sharon usually cooking for the entire group.

After retiring in December 2012 due to a breast cancer diagnosis, he returned to Albuquerque. When his cancer went into remission, he continued his ministry in New Mexico. The cancer returned, and he died on Oct. 19, 2019.[3]

"His openness and courage as he dealt with breast cancer" was noted, Stark recalled.

When he retired, the congregation sent him off with a Rootin' Tootin' Wild West party, and his final sermon here was titled "Pennies from Heaven."

"Rob was really disappointed he had to retire early," McCray said. "They really loved it here."

When Craig came on board, so did the Rev. Peggy L. Casteel as associate pastor. She remained until 2013 before moving to a church in Michigan.

***

The Rev. Eric Erickson served as a backup pastor while in semi-retirement from 2009 to 2018. He was named moderator of the Ohio Valley Presbytery in 2015, one of six from First Presbyterian to be named as such. The others were the Rev. David Liddle (1987), the Rev. Janet Lowery (1997), the Rev. Peggy Casteel (2009), Zack Ellison (2016) and current pastor the Rev. Dr. Felipe Martinez (2023).

The Rev. Peggy Casteel was hired as associate pastor around the time Rob Craig was hired in 2007.

***

One of the big building projects at the turn of the century was the stained-glass window campaign. All of the stained-glass windows had to come out because the wood surrounding them had rotted. The wood was replaced, the windows resealed and storm windows were put in so moisture didn't get in and cause problems again.

***

When Ray Hass retired as music director in 2001, he was replaced by Kyung-Won On, a native of Seoul, Korea, who had studied organ at the Indiana University School of Music. She lived in Columbus for 10 years, and was minister of music here until 2005, when she moved to First Presbyterian Church in Bentonville, Arkansas.[4]

---

[3] Robert Craig obituary, *The Republic*, Dec. 1, 2019.
[4] Clark, John. "Organist gives recital." *The Republic*, Aug. 26, 2006.

# 200 YEARS of FIRST PRESBYTERIAN CHURCH of COLUMBUS, INDIANA

Dianne Sprunger came on board in 2015 as choir director/organist.

\*\*\*

In 2010, a committee was formed with the goal of decreasing our carbon footprint by 25 percent. An expert in old buildings put together a plan. "Our building was just drafty and leaky," Vern Jorck said. "In the child care area, we heated air that was rising and going outside."

Everything was reinsulated, and all the lighting was changed to LED, which is much more efficient. All the air conditioning units had been from the 1980s; two high-efficiency furnaces were installed in the basement, and a new boiler replaced a 50-year-old one. In 2019 and 2020 the remaining air conditioning units were replaced. "We have high-efficiency heat pumps now on the child care wing; those are as efficient as you can get," Jorck said.

\*\*\*

After Rob Craig left, Scott Hill was interim pastor for three years as a search committee sought a permanent minister. Hill, originally from Milwaukee, had been working in Louisville and living in Corydon when he was called here. The rules stated the congregation could not call an interim to be the pastor, and eventually, Hill moved to Pennsylvania.

\*\*\*

In December 2015, First Presbyterian called the Rev. Dr. Felipe Martinez as its 18th and current pastor. "The search committee refused to accept the next pastor until they got it right," Stark said.

Martínez, born in Monterrey, Mexico, came to the United States in 1981 to attend Presbyterian Pan American High School in Kingsville, Texas. He obtained a Bachelor of Arts in economics and French from Austin College in Sherman, Texas, and earned his Master of Divinity and Doctor of Ministry degrees at McCormick Theological Seminary in Chicago, where one of his professors was Rob Craig. He became a U.S. citizen in 2007.

Martinez's first congregation was the First Presbyterian Church in Saint Anne, Illinois, where he served 10 years. He then served for 11 years in several capacities as staff of Whitewater Valley Presbytery, based in Indianapolis. As a bilingual and bicultural leader, he supported the presbytery's ministry with the Latino population in Indianapolis and Fort Wayne and an international partnership with Mexico and the Dominican Republic.

After a year of service at Great Rivers Presbytery in Peoria, Illinois, he felt the call back to a local congregation and came to First Presbyterian Church of Columbus, a church he knew had a long history of supporting social justice issues and interfaith dia-

Felipe Martinez

Scott Hill served as interim pastor for three years between Rob Craig and Felipe Martinez.

113

logue.

Martinez fit perfectly into the role the congregation needed.

"I thought it was absolutely the right next step for our church," Stark said. "We were at the point where we were ready to break free from some restraints. I felt he was a champion, a leader to help us follow through with it."

A strategic plan that had put into motion some more social justice initiatives was part of what drew Martinez to the church.

"Its commitment to social justice was an important reason I said yes," he said.

The strategic plan focused on:

- Everyday spirituality.
- Engaging young families.
- Assessing and addressing systemic poverty in the community.
- Clarity regarding LGBTQ issues.

"What drew my eye was the third one (systemic poverty)," he said. "I felt they were real committed to action."

The congregation's hopes in Martinez's leadership have been, and continue to be, fulfilled. Since coming here, he has worked to promote cross-cultural dialogue, honor diversity and advocate inclusion of all people in the community. He has served in committees organized by a former mayor of Indianapolis and a U.S. congressman focused on Latino issues. He currently serves on the board of the Heritage Fund of Bartholomew County and the Su Casa Columbus Board of Directors. He is serving as co-moderator of the Commission to Unify the Office of the General Assembly and the Presbyterian Church Mission of the PCUSA.

For his work in so many areas of social justice and inclusion, Martinez was named co-winner of the prestigious William R. Laws Human Rights Award for 2024. The award is presented to a member, a group of people from the community or a community organization who have made a substantial contribution to the community of Columbus in any area of human equality. Martinez received his award at the Columbus Human Rights Commission's annual dinner on July 13. The award was first presented in 1985 to J. Irwin Miller, and the following year was named for Laws. Stark won the award in 2018.

"He has a passion … no, more than a passion. He has a fire for outreach work and social justice," said Jorck.

"Felipe is definitely looking beyond the four walls, touching base with the community," Mary Ann McCray said. "One of the things he's worked on is how does he lead people to become involved? I think he sets a good example."

Among his hobbies, Martinez enjoys taking pictures and singing tenor. He and his wife, Tracy Heaton de Martinez, have two daughters, two sons and four granddaughters.

In 2023 the congregation granted Martinez a three-month sabbatical, which covered the summer months. While he was gone, Richard Safford and Brook Brown

> "He (Felipe Matrtinez) has a passion … no, more than a passion. He has a fire for outreach work and social justice."
> 
> Vern Jorck

> "One of the things he's (Martinez) worked on is how does he lead people to become involved? I think he sets a good example."
> 
> Mary Ann McCray

led our administrative ministry; Cal Brand and the deacons organized and offered pastoral care; and Dianne Sprunger, Lisa Porter, Jenny Heichelbech and the Worship Committee guided the church in some alternative worship and service experiences. Colleen Herrick and Leigh Ann Figg led the Sabbatical and Personnel Committees.

The Rev. Dr. Felipe Martinez on sabbatical in Scotland in 2023.

His sabbatical included slowing down, going on walks, exercising, reading and visiting friends in Pennsylvania, Alabama and Wisconsin. But it also included a six-week period in Europe, where he spent time learning, traveling, discovering and photographing. He spent a week's spiritual retreat in an abbey in Iona, Scotland, and visited Paris, London and Edinburgh. His wife, Tracy, met him for the final two weeks, and they visited Scotland and Ireland.[5]

Martinez was the third pastor to take a sabbatical; the others were David Liddle and Bill Laws.

\*\*\*

The hiring of Martinez came while the congregation was in the process of becoming a More Light church, one supportive of LGBTQ+ people. First Presbyterian made the announcement that it had become a More Light church at its Aug. 21, 2016 service.[6] The strategic plan had identified the move as something desired by the congregation earlier, and there had been discussions for months beforehand to decide exactly what this meant. Not that everyone agreed; the move was seen as controversial by some members, who chose to leave the church over it.

But the decision also led to others coming on board or becoming even more committed than they had previously been.

"We seem blessed with more people than we lost with the decision to be a welcoming and affirming church," said Cal Brand. "I hope being a 'woke' congregation doesn't make others feel excluded or judged. But it seemed to me to be a good place to be."

"That strategic plan led us in the way that led us to Felipe," said Stark, who chaired that strategic plan committee. "Before that, there was some dancing around the issues, and after the strategic plan, we had the outcomes, and we needed to decide what to do."

More Light Presbyterian churches engage more than 330 congregations and thousands of individuals in the Presbyterian Church (USA), enabling Presbyterians to lead LGBTQIA+ service and advocacy in communities nationwide. More Light's mission has always been to empower and equip individuals and

> "We seem blessed with more people than we lost with the decision to be a welcoming and affirming church."
>
> Cal Brand

---

5  First Presbyterian Church of Columbus, Indiana, Annual Report, 2023
6  Religion news: First Presbyterian. *The Republic*, Aug. 20, 2016.

# 200 YEARS of FIRST PRESBYTERIAN CHURCH of COLUMBUS, INDIANA

> "When we welcome others, we welcome Christ; when we bring together people who are divided, we are doing God's reconciling work."
>
> Presbyterian Church (USA)

congregations to welcome LGBTQIA+ people.[7] This followed a couple of landmark decisions by the denomination. LGBTQ people could be ordained as pastors in PCUSA as of 2011, and PCUSA pastors were approved to officiate LGBTQ weddings in 2015.

The church now has an Open and Affirming committee, which promotes the rights of the LGBTQ+ community.

\*\*\*

In April 2021 the Session voted to have our church become a Matthew 25 congregation. The invitation focuses on Matthew 25: 31-46, the parable of the sheep and goats in which Jesus makes clear that what we do and how we treat others matters to God. As of mid-2024, 1,225 congregations have embraced the vision.

"When we welcome others, we welcome Christ; when we bring together people who are divided, we are doing God's reconciling work. We are called to serve Jesus by contributing to the well-being of the most vulnerable in all societies – rural and urban, small and large, young and not-so-young. From affordable housing to community gardens to equitable educational and employment opportunities to healing from addiction and mental illness to enacting policy change – there is not just one way to be a part of the Matthew 25 movement."[8]

The Matthew 25 Initiative has three areas of focus:

- Building congregational vitality by challenging people and congregations to deepen their faith and get actively and joyfully engaged with their community and the world.

- Dismantling structural racism by advocating and acting to break down the systems, practices and thinking that underlie discrimination, bias, prejudice and oppression of people of color.

- Eradicating systemic poverty by working to change laws, policies, plans and structures in our society that perpetuate economic exploitation of people who are poor.

"We touch on all three," Martinez said of his church, "especially eradicating systemic poverty through the lens of housing. We've beat the drum of Permanent Supportive Housing for some time, looking for a way to partner with the city and social service agencies. Because that's the only way it's going to happen."

\*\*\*

The Laws Peacemaking series was created in 1993 to honor Bill Laws' ideals. The first speaker was John M. Fife, who was moderator of the General Assembly in 1992 to 1993. Several nationally known peacemakers have graced us with their insight. The series has been held annually, with a few exceptions. The 2006 event featured jazz pianist

Lee Hamilton has twice been the guest speaker for the Laws Peacemaking series.

---

7  More Light Presbyterian website, ttps://mlp.org/about-us/
8  Presbyterian Church (USA) Matthew 25, https://www.presbyterianmission.org/ministries/matthew-25/

## 200 YEARS of FIRST PRESBYTERIAN CHURCH of COLUMBUS, INDIANA

Henry Pickens instead of a speaker. The series was not conducted during the coronavirus pandemic.

Speakers:

1993: John M. Fife
1994: Dr. Richard Joseph
1995: Lee Hamilton
1996: James and Kathleen McGinnis
1997: Elise Boulding
1998: Hal Saunders
1999: Henry Schacht
2000: Matthew Fox
2001: David R. Franz
2002: Robert J. Young
2003: the Rev. Joan Brown Campbell
2004: Dr. Paul Zeitz
2005: the Rev. Philip Gulley
2006: None. Jazz pianist Henry Pickens performed.
2007: the Rev. Carol Wickersham
2008: the Rev. Cynthia Campbell
2009: None
2010: the Rev. Daniel Groody
2011: the Rev. Mitri Raheb
2012: Stephanie Paulsell
2013: None
2014: the Rev. Allan Boesak
2015: None
2016: Lee Hamilton
2017: Richard Lugar
2018: Fran Quigley
2019-2022: None (COVID)
2023: the Rev. Adam Russell Taylor

This event is co-sponsored by First Presbyterian Church, Interfaith Forum Columbus and Presbytery of Ohio Valley Mission Partnership.

Above: The Rev. Dr. Mitri Raheb, pastor of Christmas Lutheran Church in Bethlehem, was the speaker at First Presbyterian's Laws Peacemaking series in 2011. Right: This part of Dar Al-Kalima University houses the culinary school.

\*\*\*

The congregation has expressed its solidarity with Palestinian college Dar Al-Kalima University in Bethlehem and supported the creation of the school's library. In 2011, the Rev. Dr. Mitri Raheb, pastor of the Christmas Lutheran Church in Bethlehem and president of the Diyar Consortium, was the speaker at the annual Laws Peacekeeping Lecture, held at the church.

\*\*\*

The 144-foot-high steeple was given a new copper surface in 2007. Elizabethtown's NRS Inc. spearheaded the $350,000 project that took a little over a month to complete and replaced the copper surface that had been installed in the 1920s. That project replaced the original slate.

The cross-topped section of the church was a source of pride for members, according to member

# 200 YEARS of FIRST PRESBYTERIAN CHURCH of COLUMBUS, INDIANA

The 144-foot-high steeple was given a new copper surface in 2007.

Jeff Crump. "I think church steeples were a landmark for people in the old days," he said.[9]

A copper Celtic cross and weathervane were affixed to the top of the steeple in summer 2016, matching an old one that had been damaged by high winds in the spring. A sculptor from Nashville, Tennessee, made the new cross, which was installed by ABC Construction.[10]

***

In 2011, First Presbyterian donated $10,000 seed money to help start Hoosier Interfaith Power & Light, a nonprofit agency focused on providing environmental advocacy, education, energy innovation and community works. In 2022, that group merged with two other similar agencies to form Faith in Place, an affiliate of HIPL that covers Illinois, Indiana and Wisconsin. The church is giving Faith in Place nearly $90,000 this year, $45,000 from Mission Support. FPC member Eric Riddle is development coordinator with Faith in Place.

***

The church, like most of the United States, was significantly affected by the coronavirus pandemic, which hit in earnest in April 2020.

In-person services were halted for a time, and masks were required upon return when the Centers for Disease Control and Prevention status warranted it. Sometimes, services were conducted in the parking lot north of the church with attendees bringing lawn chairs. When indoor services returned, every other pew was off limits and the "passing of the peace" was done with nods, elbow taps or some other gesture instead of handshakes, grasps or hugs.

The preschool classrooms' parents parties and graduations went on hold. Choir and music were severely limited, though hymnals were sent to the homes of those who wished them.

Services were also put online for those who didn't want to come in person. YouTube and Facebook became the go-to for some, and those methods of accessing services are still used by many, some of whom are either homebound or are watching from miles away and wouldn't get to participate any other way.

---

9  Blair, Brian. "Spiritual face-lift: Steeple resurfaced at First Presbyterian for $350K in month." *The Republic*, April 28, 2007.
10  Blair, Brian. "Brand New: First Presbyterian installs Celtic cross on steeple." *The Republic*, July 28, 2016.

# 200 YEARS of FIRST PRESBYTERIAN CHURCH of COLUMBUS, INDIANA

> "The pandemic kind of pushed us to catch up to the 21st century. … It made us get creative in how we get the message out."
>
> Zack Ellison

One Easter, Martinez and his wife, Tracy, conducted a service from the Laws Room. They were the only ones there; everyone else was watching online.

"It was a real hardship on the staff; I think it took a toll," McCray said.

The effects have been mixed.

"A plus was that it put us into broadcasting," said Ellison, who added that years ago, churches used to have their own radio stations and/or broadcast their services live on the radio. First Presbyterian used to record services that were available in the church library for anyone who wanted to listen. But "the pandemic kind of pushed us to catch up to the 21st century. … It made us get creative in how we get the message out," he said. In addition to services being provided online, meetings and adult fellowship education classes were held remotely via Zoom, and that option still exists for many meetings.

"In some ways, that (online presence) was lifesaving," Stark said.

"This congregation pivoted during the pandemic to continue to worship, adapt to a new reality, created a streaming capacity that is professional to keep our people connected," Martinez said. "And it did so without a drop in financial resources, which is commendable."

The downside is that numbers for in-person events aren't back to pre-pandemic levels. And that's a concern for some.

"There's a disconnect," Stark said. "Getting back into the sanctuary is hard. People can work at home,

Among the technological advancements in the sanctuary in recent years have been the addition of streaming services online and the introduction of a screen at the front. // Paul J. Hoffman

and they can still connect with other people through these other things. But something is missing (when they don't meet face to face)."

"We're almost two congregations now: one in the sanctuary and one online," McCray said. "I feel like we're losing something. I'm not saying we should stop streaming; it's a real plus. But it's also a minus because we're not all getting together.

"I don't care how much you tune in, I don't think you're as well-informed if you're not here. You can't write everything in a newsletter, just like you can't say everything from the pulpit."

"It feels better to get back and talk to people, to get some social interaction" Ellison said. "And church is a whole lot about social interaction."

Tech advancements predated the pandemic though. Previously, long-range planning sessions with a consultant had put a video screen on the wall behind the pulpit for the first time. The screen is used to project announcements, song lyrics and prayers during the service, as well as videos that are incorporated into the services. "I said, 'Really? We're going to put a screen on the wall? Is there going to be a bouncing ball under the words? No way!'" McCray said. "Well, never say, 'No way.'"

In partnership with the church foundation, security cameras were added to the building entrances, classroom windows and doors to enhance safety for everyone who uses our building.

\*\*\*

The congregation supported a nondiscrimination ordinance, passed by the City Council in 2015, which at that time was amended to include sexual orientation and gender identity. The policy states, in part: "A written or unwritten act, policy, practice or system which excludes an individual from equal opportunities on the basis of sex or because of sex, sexual orientation, or gender identity in any terms or conditions of employment, education, public accommodations, credit or housing, shall be considered a discriminatory practice."

\*\*\*

A capital campaign OK'd in 2017 raised $175,000. Along with a matching grant from the FPC Foundation, the money paid for:

- Expansion of the columbarium.
- Rebuilding the north parking lot.
- Replacing most trees (unsuitable trees had been planted, and some were too close to the building) on our property and fixing sidewalks.
- Reeves and Crump room improvements.
- Tithing 10 percent for local mission (on a set-aside fund).

> "I'm not saying we should stop streaming; it's a real plus. But it's also a minus because we're not all getting together."
>
> Mary Ann McCray

\*\*\*

The church was one of the organizations that combined in 2016 to secure an emergency homeless shelter. Brighter Days Housing opened that October in the former Columbus Township fire truck maintenance facility at 421 S. Mapleton St. The 36-bed facility, split into two bunk areas separated by gender, is operated by Love Chapel, an outreach program of the Ecumenical Assembly of Bartholomew County Churches. Columbus Township is the landlord and leases the building to Love Chapel for one dollar a year. The cost to renovate the building was expected to be about $300,000, but roughly two-thirds of that was donated. The facility is for those 18 and older who are homeless and is open overnight, with a continental breakfast served.[11]

\*\*\*

Congregation members Roger Brinkman and Dr. Sherm Franz were two of the catalysts behind an effort to help stem drug abuse here. As members of the Community Mental Health Team, they provided guidance and leadership as the team sponsored an Opioid Summit at Columbus Regional Hospital in spring 2016, when leaders and elected officials discussed the opioid crisis. A community-wide response was championed, and the effort eventually became the Alliance for Substance Abuse Progress of Bartholomew County. The mission of ASAP is to lead, identify and implement prevention and recovery system solutions to substance misuse in Bartholomew County.

\*\*\*

Doug Sprunger started an outreach in 2019 to provide free firewood to lower-income families who depend on wood to heat their homes. Sprunger continues to lead the WoodWeShare ministry.

On Faith in Action Day in 2023, a Sunday where members help people in the community in lieu of attending church services, the WoodWeShare program split, delivered and stacked a ton of wood. At the time, there were three families heating with WoodWeShare wood and another family receiving occasional assistance.[12]

\*\*\*

The Granny Connection supports grandmothers in Africa who are raising children orphaned by AIDS. The organization is dedicated to encouraging self-sufficiency in communities affected by the disease through micro loans, business training and health care services. Granny Connection sells glazed pecans and has conducted various fundraisers over the years. The idea for creating a charity such as this came to founder and First Presbyterian member Ann Jones after she visited Africa in 2003 and saw the impact of HIV/AIDS there. At the time, 17 million Africans had died of AIDS-related illnesses, and it was killing one African every 13 seconds on average. Jones, who along with her husband, Bill, has advocated for many worthwhile causes both here and abroad, vowed to continue the fight. "The issue isn't going to go away for a long time," she said at the time.[13]

It hasn't. In 2022 an estimated 25.6 million Africans were living with HIV, nearly seven times the number in North and South America combined.[14]

The Granny Connection sells glazed pecans to raise money to support grandmothers in Africa who are raising children orphaned by AIDS. // Paul J. Hoffman

---

11  McClure, Julie. "'Brighter' future: Generosity from community helps fill need for emergency housing." *The Republic*. Sept. 28, 2016.
12  "WoodWeShare Ministries." First Presbyterian Church 2023 Annual Report
13  Werner, Nick. "Images of AIDS: Columbus woman returns from African trip, hopes to raise awareness of disease that's devastating continent." *The Republic,* June 1, 2003.
14  World Health Organization, https://cdn.who.int/media/docs/default-source/hq-hiv-hepatitis-and-stis-library/j0294-who-hiv-epi-factsheet-v7.pdf.

> "The leadership at the church feels that it is important to honor the talent of the African American composers and lyricists who created these spirituals decades ago, even though there is no way now to get royalties to them."
>
> Felipe Martinez

***

In May 2024 Dianne Sprunger retired as organist after nine years on the job. She had also been choir director. Jordan Lewis was hired as organist upon her retirement. In later years, she kept the organ duties, while Jenny Heichelbech took choir director duties. We have also been blessed by having the Livin' by Faith band, a bell choir with a donation of bells from the former North Christian Church and special music on many occasions.[15]

***

In 2021, the preschool applied for and was awarded the Build, Learn, Grow Stabilization grant, which helped strengthen and support early childhood programming in the state. In 2023, we continued to make improvements to the building, classroom spaces and programming. Upgrades to the education wing classrooms included new drywall, paint and screens for the sliding doors. Carpets were rebound, and mulch was added to the playground on the far north end of the property.

We also got a Paycheck Protection loan that turned into a grant to pay our staff to keep the preschool open. Some went to the church but most to the preschool.

***

Within the past year, we've made some significant contributions to the community.

This year, First Presbyterian started donating $100 annually to the African American Fund of Bartholomew County to honor African American musicians whose hymns are sung occasionally in worship. Many of these old hymns are in the public domain, which means the writers no longer receive royalties. First Presbyterian, like all churches, pays licensing fees for music used in worship that has not entered the public domain yet.

"The leadership at the church feels that it is important to honor the talent of the African American composers and lyricists who created these spirituals decades ago, even though there is no way now to get royalties to them," wrote Felipe Martinez in a letter to the editor of *The Republic*. "As a symbolic gesture of gratitude, the church has started" donating to the fund. First Presbyterian is encouraging other area churches to do the same.[16]

***

The church's Matthew 25 efforts continue to focus on housing. In 2023, the vision for our work came into sharper focus, as the committee decided to catalyze a process that would eventually lead to the creation of Permanent Supportive Housing in Columbus. That effort will require collaboration with social service agencies, city government, and public and private partners. We are grateful for the leadership and passion of Glyn Price, Alan Kilbarger and Sarah Kilbarger-Stumpff and the Housing Committee.

***

---

15  First Presbyterian Church of Columbus, Indiana, Annual Report, 2023
16  "Church provides offering for African American spirituals." *The Republic*, June 15, 2024.

The Afghan families supported by the community continue to make strides in becoming acclimated to the United States. Some of the original seven families have moved from Columbus, being able to resettle nearer to relatives already living in the States. The Karimi family, whom the church has sponsored, is feeling more settled. Both parents are working, and the children are doing well in school.

\*\*\*

The preschool won an award at the start of 2023 for the "Best Preschool in Town" through The Republic newspaper. It awarded $18,750 in scholarships for the 2023-2024 school year and once again began offering a three-week summer program for more than 50 children. The preschool was honored with the 10-year Paths to Quality award in September. This was a huge milestone for us as it reflects our having met rigorous standards and requirements in our field for over 10 years.

Adult Fellowship Education encourages everyday spirituality, fellowship with the church community with a special focus on young adults, and social justice issues through formal and informal sessions. This was accomplished in 2023 through regular programming, including Virtual Coffee Fellowship, Adult Sunday School Education, Patio Parties Plus and Fellowship Pitch-In Meals. Along with several "traditional" patio parties, original events included a Bike and Brunch, Brown County Hike, Trivia Night, Euchre Night, Caribbean Cooking Class, Flute, Piano and Dessert, and more. Participation increased from previous years and was more successful at bringing in participants from outside our congregation.

The Children's Nurture Committee was led by Tonja Gerardy the first half of the year, with Jen Riddle

*Children perform a skit during worship service.*

serving as our full-time director of children, youth and young adults the second half of the year. The committee recruits and trains teachers and helpers for Kids Church. It supported restructuring Communion Sundays to be a more kid-friendly intergenerational service. Tween Time, a monthly youth group for Grades 3 to 6, focused on Matthew 25 in our monthly activities. FPC participated in planning and in the daily activities of the first Interfaith Peace Camp, sponsored by Interfaith Columbus member congregations. The committee also holds kid-friendly events during the year. Children's service projects included the holiday chicken fundraiser, where $394 was raised for flocks of chickens for families in need. The Tween Time group made a tied fleece blanket to donate to Sweet Dreams.

The Youth Nurture Committee conducted the Christian Education/Faith Formation: Preparing for Youth Sunday '23. On Youth Sunday, we dedicated our new youth banner, Growing in The Spirit, designed and created by Marietta Macy. In the fall, we began a new confirmation class with eight students, each with an adult mentor. Our Whole Lives comprehensive, inclusive sexuality education for Grades 7 to 9 was conduct-

# 200 YEARS of FIRST PRESBYTERIAN CHURCH of COLUMBUS, INDIANA

ed during the 2022-23 school year. Service projects the youth engaged in were Hot Meals, the Souper Bowl of Caring that raised $435 for Love Chapel, a Pentecost offering that raised $1,348, $539 of which went to Book Buddies. They collected hats, gloves and children's toys for Hot Meals guests. We also collected $1,250 for latrines to be built in communities without such amenities, which will greatly reduce assault on women and community illness. The annual Christmas party included caroling and dessert with our neighbors at the Armory Apartments.

The Social Justice Committee held a two-day workshop for adults on Interrupting Racism for Children, formed a separate Housing Committee to bring Permanent Supportive Housing to Columbus, and advocated against the anti-LGBTQ+ bills introduced in the Indiana House in 2023. The Open & Affirming Subcommittee hosted a tent at the Columbus Pride Festival, to convey that "God's doors are open to all." We donated our 25 percent share of the Peace and Global Witness Offering to the Presbyterian Disaster Assistance Fund specifically for Palestine. We continue to support Bright Stars of Bethlehem, which provides higher education opportunities for Muslims and Christians in Palestine, and the Power of Love Foundation. We also support two mission co-workers and 17 community-serving organizations. The 2023 funds distributed totaled $34,500.

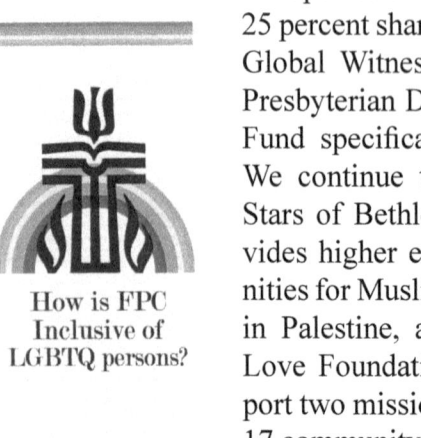

*Anthony Merida, left, has helped organize First Presbyterian's booth at Columbus Pride. Here he is with Sherry Stark, David Tiede, and their dog, Maisie, in 2023.*

**How is FPC Inclusive of LGBTQ persons?**

*February 2015*

The Sweet Dreams Ministry helped several children this past year by providing new twin beds complete with all the bedding. This is our sixth year providing beds for children who live in Bartholomew County.

A goal of the Worship Committee in 2023 was to invite and include many voices, perspectives and forms of expression, representing the diversity of our faith community. Many contributed singing, reading, art, slides, tech expertise, dance, stories, rhythm and more, especially during the pastor's sabbatical. We helped Joy Basa King and the deacons organize our inaugural Day of Service, in which we worshipped God with meditative prayer, gutter cleaning, sorting, electrical wiring, cooking and baking, and sitting with our siblings and neighbors in fellowship and solidarity. We also had a tremendous group of 10 adults attend the Montreat Worship and Music Conference in the North Carolina mountains. We purchased projectable Glory to God hymnal slides that include musical notes as well as the words. We also started including

# 200 YEARS of FIRST PRESBYTERIAN CHURCH of COLUMBUS, INDIANA

kindergarten to sixth-grade children on Communion Sundays for the whole service, rather than having them leave for Kids Church.

The deacons connect with and pray for the individuals and families on their deacon member lists, coordinate ushering and lead several fellowship events each year, including Deacons & Donuts, Easter Brunch, church picnic and Consecration Brunch.

The Presbyterian Foundation of Columbus, Indiana, serves the religious, educational and charitable needs of the congregation. The 2023 annual unrestricted grant funds available total $176,394.74.

We also welcomed Missy Burton as our financial administrative assistant, as Christy Jerman ended her role with us after seven years. Burton is well-known to the church, as she is also the financial and human resources assistant for our preschool.

As of the end of 2023, we had 487 members. We have three full-time employees (the Rev. Dr. Felipe Martinez, Brook Brown and Jen Riddle) and four part-time employees (Jenny Heichelbech, Missy Burton, Jordan Lewis and Wayne Huff). The preschool has 27 staff members, and nearly all 186 spaces are filled.

\*\*\*

And now we're in our 200th year. That's the longest any congregation has continuously served Bartholomew County without a change in denomination. Two of our neighbors are older, but both have switched denominations. Old Union Church of Christ north of Columbus started in 1816 as New Light Christian Church. In 1931, it became a Congregational Christian church, and 30 years later a Church of Christ. New Hope Christian Church between Columbus and Taylorsville got off the ground as a Baptised (Baptist) Church of Christ at Columbus. A year later, it was New Hope Baptised Church, then took on its current affiliation in 1832.

200 YEARS of FIRST PRESBYTERIAN CHURCH of COLUMBUS, INDIANA

# Our Bicentennial

**Preparations for our bicentennial** celebration began well before the calendar turned to 2024. Our Bicentennial Committee, headed by Sherry Stark and Rachel McCarver, planned a slew of activities to honor our past and build our legacy.

One of the goals for these events was to involve and enrich the community that we've partnered with throughout the years.

The project that will have the longest and most powerful impact is the FPC Bicentennial Legacy Project, which will make a difference in the lives of our downtown neighbors, some of whom are struggling to reach economic self-sufficiency. The funds being collected will be held in a permanently endowed fund at Heritage Fund – the Community Foundation of Bartholomew County. Grants awarded will be determined by Lincoln-Central Neighborhood Family Center, which works with other community groups in serving and encouraging individuals and families. Our goal was to raise $100,000. The First Presbyterian Church Foundation has agreed to match each dollar given up to $100,000. Lilly Endowment has agreed to match gifts donated to our project on a dollar-for-dollar basis.

Besides the Legacy Project, several other projects and celebrations were planned for 2024:

- On one Sunday per month throughout the year, a member of the Bicentennial Committee discussed an aspect of the 200-year history or celebration activities during church services.
- Adult nurture classes about Bill and Ellen Laws and Sarah Hunt were presented by Janet Lowery.
- Anthony Merida's artistic handiwork put special lights in all the windows of the sanctuary.
- Columbus North student Claire Davis produced a video on First Presbyterian for her

Lisa Porter speaks in the video produced by Columbus North senior Claire Davis that was shown in lieu of a sermon during the June 9, 2024, service.

# 200 YEARS of FIRST PRESBYTERIAN CHURCH of COLUMBUS, INDIANA

Left: Tracy Heaton de Martinez enjoys ice cream at our ice cream social on July 21, 2024. Above: The mandolin concert on Aug. 4, 2024.

- senior project. This video was shown in lieu of a sermon during the June 9 service.
- Downtown neighbors were invited to join us in an ice cream social in the parking lot north of the church on July 21 after the service.
- This book, which stands on the shoulders of Carol Berkey's 175th anniversary book of 1999.
- A special mandolin concert was held during service on Aug. 4.
- We will have a special service on Sunday morning, Sept. 15, to celebrate our bicentennial, with the 226th General Assembly (2024) Co-Moderator the Rev. Tony Larson preaching, and with Ohio Valley Presbytery Executive the Rev. Susan McGhee and Lincoln Trails Synod Executive the Rev. Sara Dingman as our special guests.
- The big 200-year party was planned for the afternoon of Sept. 15 at Donner Park. The community-wide bicentennial celebration will have the Rev. Dr. Felipe Martinez as emcee, while speakers include Columbus Mayor Mary Ferdon and Fairview Presbyterian pastor the Rev. Elizabeth Kilpatrick. There will also be music by members of the band Cottonpatch, as well as games, activities for kids, refreshments and more.

We want to give a special thanks to the Bicentennial Committee for all its hard work and dedication to these projects.

**Bicentennial Committee:**

Sherry Stark, co-chair

Rachel McCarver, co-chair

Bonnie Boatwright

Zack Ellison

Paul Hoffman

The Rev. Dr. Felipe N. Martinez

Mary Ann McCray

Anthony Merida

Kelleigh Staley

Doug Wray

# Our Future

**Two hundred years** after John M. Dickey presided over the chartering of First Presbyterian Church in Columbus, Indiana, we look back at what our congregation has done. We're pleased.

But we're not so satisfied that we'll stop pushing onward with the message of God's love through our own actions and taking personal responsibility to

---

> "I think we're on the brink of some wonderful growth and impact ... It's taken time, and no one is going to wave a magic wand. But we've realized we all need to step up and make a difference as individuals."
>
> Sherry Stark

---

make the community in which we live a better place for all.

So where do we go from here?

"I think we're on the brink of some wonderful growth and impact," Sherry Stark said. "The community, along with COVID, we went through a fallow time. It's taken time, and no one is going to wave a magic wand. But we've realized we all need to step up and make a difference as individuals."

Longtime members see First Presbyterian continuing to be "a church that tries to be a supporter of justice and inclusivity," the Rev. Felipe Martinez said, summing up the feelings of many. "Connecting with other people of faith and others to advocate for people in need."

Some of the social justice initiatives the church started are ongoing and thriving; there are more to come.

In celebration of our bicentennial, FPC has established a permanently endowed fund that will offer grants as a "hand up" to downtown neighbors and other qualified individuals. Each grant will be intended to be a "barrier buster" that allows people to move toward self-sufficiency. The focus will be on downtown neighbors, but all in Bartholomew County are eligible. Lincoln-Central Neighborhood Family Center, working with other community groups, will identify the recipients.

Examples of possible grants include:

- Educational funds (training, tuition, supplies).
- Small business expenses (necessary equipment).
- Households close to losing self-sufficiency.

The funds will be administered by the Heritage

> "I don't know how you can believe that inclusion and social justice isn't the right thing. That's Christianity; that's Christ in action. We try to live that out … and I think Felipe is the right person to lead us."
>
> Vern Jorck

Fund – the Community Foundation of Bartholomew County.

"This congregation is going to make a big impact with the Legacy Project," Martinez said. "There are no funds like this that are available to people who want to start a business or get training. If we get our ducks in a row, we can provide significant money each year in perpetuity."

Another project that the church is working on is bringing Permanent Supportive Housing to Columbus to reduce homelessness here. The congregation's housing committee has met with local individuals who are or have been homeless, gained valuable information from agencies and other communities that have erected Permanent Supportive Housing, and met with potential community partners.

"This congregation will make a difference in the community with Permanent Supportive Housing," Martinez said.

As for attendance, perhaps gone are the days of packed sanctuaries every Sunday. The downward trend in membership and attendance started before the COVID-19 pandemic, but that probably exacerbated the circumstances.

"While the pandemic may be over, the impact on church membership is still being felt," said the Rev. J. Herbert Nelson II, stated clerk of the Presbyterian Church (USA) General Assembly, in a May 1, 2023, report from the PC(USA). The report said the denomination had lost more than 100 congregations and 53,000 members in 2022 and lost more than 700 congregations and 340,000 members since 2016.

One of the Presbyterian churches to close in recent years was in Bartholomew County; Grammer Presbyterian Church ended its 114-year run when it shut its doors in 2021.

"Churches in general are in decline as far as membership mode goes, and that's every denomination," said Zack Ellison. "Young people who want to go to church typically go to get entertained. That's why you have the mega churches and bands and guitars. And if you don't have young membership, you're going to go out of business."

He added that many people who consider themselves Christians today don't attend church regularly or don't consider themselves members of a congregation. So while official membership may be down, that doesn't necessarily mean people aren't still interested in the Christian message and living it.

Due to declining membership, some churches have consolidated. Perhaps at some point, Ellison wondered, would First Presbyterian and Fairlawn merge?

One positive finding the May 2023 PC(USA) report showed was that more than 20 new worshipping communities were added in 2022.

"In the midst of the lower numbers, we continue to find encouragement in that new worshipping communities are still on the increase," Nelson stated.

# 200 YEARS of FIRST PRESBYTERIAN CHURCH of COLUMBUS, INDIANA

Ellison feels there are issues in which the church as an organization can be an instrument of progress. "There's still work to be done where church plays a big role in it, like human rights."

Vern Jorck agrees.

"I think we're going in the right direction as far as inclusion goes," Jorck said. "I don't know how you can believe that inclusion and social justice isn't the right thing. That's Christianity; that's Christ in action. We try to live that out … and I think Felipe is the right person to lead us."

"I think our best days are ahead of us," Stark said.

# Our Ministers

**Lead ministers (not including interim)**

1824-28 — Occasionally supplied by John M. Dickey, James H. Johnston, Samuel Gregg, John F. Crowe, and others.

1829 — Eliphalet Kent, two Sabbaths a month

1830 — Hilary Patrick and Henry Little, more or less regularly

1831 — W. W. Wood, occasionally

1832-33 — Hilary Patrick, occasionally

1833-35 — Michael A. Remley, regularly

1836 — John M. Dickey, at times, and William Stimson for six months

1837 — Records of John M. Dickey holding some services

1838 — David Monfort, regularly

1839 — John M. Dickey and James G. Monfort, occasionally

1840-42 — Windsor A. Smith, regularly, with John M. Dickey and Henry Little, occasionally

1842-49 — Benjamin M. Nyce, more or less regularly, with Henry Little, James H. Johnston, John F. Crowe, James Galliher, Daniel Latimore, occasionally

1849-50 — Charles Merwin

1850-53 — James Brownlee (first installed minister)

1853-70 — Ninian S. Dickey

1870-83 — Alexander Parker

1884-86 — George S. J. Browne

1887-92 — S. Robinson Frazier

1892-96 — Fenwick W. Fraser

1896-1900 — Frank C. Hood

1901-06 — Charles G. Richards

1906-09 — Amos K. Mattingly

1910-32 — Alexander E. Sharp Sr.

1932-39 — Alexander E. Sharp Jr.

1940-49 — Harold W. Turpin

1950-76 — William R. Laws Jr.

1976-82 — Warner M. Bailey

   Note: Laws and Bailey served as co-pastors from 1973-76

1982-97 — David M. Liddle

1999-2007 — Richard Underdahl-Peirce

2007-2012 — Robert H. Craig

2015-present — Felipe N. Martinez

**Other ministers**

1946-61 — Theodore Hunt, Minister of Music

1959-64 — Edward Wicklein, Assistant Minister

1961-2001 — Ramon L. Hass, Minister of Music

1965-69 — Barnett Shepherd, Assistant and Associate Minister

1968-72 — Jerry Kerns, Associate Minister

1973-75 — Warner M. Bailey, Associate Minister

1977-82 — David M. Liddle, Associate Minister

1982-87 — Frances Unsell, Associate Minister

1987-99 — Janet Lowery, Associate Minister

1998-99 — Norie Erickson, Head of Staff

2001-05 — Ruth Billington, Associate Minister

2007-13 — Peggy Casteel, Associate Minister

# About the Author

Paul J. Hoffman is an author, publisher, journalist, actor, and a member of First Presbyterian Church in Columbus, Indiana.

A native of Wisconsin, he spent 34 years in journalism, working as a sportswriter, news editor and nearly 20 years as special publications editor in Franklin and Columbus, Indiana, for Home News Enterprises and its successor, AIM Media Indiana.

Paul's first book, *Murder in Wauwatosa: The Mysterious Death of Buddy Schumacher*, was published in 2012 by The History Press. It is the true story of the disappearance of an 8-year-old boy in 1925 and the subsequent investigation into the boy's murder. *Wicked Columbus, Indiana*, published in 2017 by the same publisher, tells the true tales of some of that city's more notorious stories.

He is the president and owner of PathBinder Publishing LLC, which he purchased in 2020.

He has also worked as an extra in two movies, as well as acted in several community theater productions, including a starring role in *Kalamazoo* at Willow Leaves of Hope in February 2023.

He is a graduate of Leadership Johnson County (2016) and former co-chair of LJC's liaison committee, and ran for Columbus City Council in 2023 and Bartholomew County Council in 2022.

He enjoys walking and raising money for Huntington's Disease research.

Paul lives in Columbus with his wife, children's author Kimberly S. Hoffman. They have six adult children and a granddaughter.